Welcome

Editor
Nadine Hawkins
NHAWKINS@DCTHOMSON.CO.UK

Content Editor
Emma Hayley Rinaldi
ERINALDI@DCTHOMSON.CO.UK

Since he was just three years old, Charles has known that one day he would be King. And in September 2022, upon the death of his beloved mother, who celebrated a record-breaking reign and immense popularity, he became our new Monarch.

This special collector's issue celebrates the life of our new King and delves into the man behind the crown.

From his early childhood and the special bond he enjoyed with his parents and grandparents, to his education and time in the military, we examine the King's extensive and impressive work with the charities that are so close to his heart and how he instilled the importance of giving back to his sons.

We also look at the era-defining moments of his life so far that have led him on his journey to become King. And the part his loving wife Camilla, and soon to be Queen Consort, played on that journey.

Details of Coronation traditions of the past will also be revealed, alongside facts about the jewels and regalia we can expect His Majesty to wear for the momentous occasion.

So without further ado, we present this fascinating look at the past, present and future of His Majesty, King Charles III.

CONTENTS

22

38

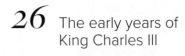

44

WITH THANKS

Design
Lindsay McFadyen

Picture Editor
Karen Milne

Picture researcher
Gillian Petrie

Chief Revenue Officer
Andy Williams
anwilliams@dcthomson.co.uk

Head of advertising
Craig French
cfrench@dcthomson.co.uk

Platinum shop Partnerships
Jacqui Hunter
jhunter@dcthomson.co.uk

Insights and Innovations
Karen Campbell

Head of Circulation
Iain McKenzie
imckenzie@dcthomson.co.uk

Subscriptions, Sales and Customer Services
0800 318846
shop@dcthomson.co.uk

Published in Great Britain by D C Thomson & Co. Ltd., 185 Fleet Street, London EC4A 2HS. © D C Thomson & Co. Ltd., 2022. While every reasonable care will be taken, neither D C Thomson & Co Ltd, nor its agents accept liability for loss or damage to colour transparencies or any other material submitted to this publication. We will only use the data provided to contact people in relation to competitions or letters. You can find our privacy policy at www.dctmedia.co.uk/privacy-policy/ Subscribers customer service & sales: shop@dcthomson.co.uk Freephone 0800 318846/+44 (0)1382 575580. We are committed to journalism of the highest standards and abide by the Editors' Code of Practice which is enforced by the Independent Press Standards Organisation (IPSO). If you have a complaint, you can email us at readerseditor@dcthomson.co.uk or write to the Readers' Editor at My Weekly, DC Thomson Ltd, 2 Albert Square, Dundee, DD1 1DD. Distributed by Frontline Ltd, Stuart House, St John's St, Peterborough, Cambridgeshire PE1 5DD. Tel: +44 (0) 1733 555161. Website: www.frontlinedistribution.co.uk. EXPORT DISTRIBUTION (excluding AU and NZ) Seymour Distribution Ltd, 2 East Poultry Avenue, London EC1A 9PT Tel: +44(0)20 7429 4000 Fax: +44(0)20 7429 4001. Website: www.seymour.co.uk. EU Representative Office: DC Thomson & Co Ltd, c/o Findmypast Ireland, Irishtown, Athlone, Co. Westmeath, N37 XP5

OUR NEW
Monarch

HISTORIAN **DR. TRACY BORMAN** DISCUSSES THE
ACCESSION OF KING CHARLES III WITH **CLAIRE SAUL**

"As The Queen herself did with such unswerving devotion, I too now solemnly pledge myself, throughout the remaining time God grants me, to uphold the Constitutional principles at the heart of our nation. And wherever you may live in the United Kingdom, or in the Realms and territories across the world, and whatever may be your background or beliefs, I shall endeavour to serve you with loyalty, respect and love, as I have throughout my life."

King Charles III, September 2022

By the arrival of our eighth decade, the chapter has usually closed on our working years and their attendant challenges and demands on our daily lives. We embrace a period of more personal fulfilment, enjoying more time with family, friendship groups, life-enriching activities, travel and, perhaps, a more sedate pace of existence.

Yet, at the age of 73, the Prince of Wales became 'Charles R' in September last year. Older Monarchs haven't necessarily made the most successful Monarchs, as historian Tracy Borman illustrates in her book *Crown & Sceptre: A New History of the British Monarchy from William the Conqueror to Charles III*, and time will tell how we will reflect on his reign. But the tide of public approval is certainly currently in his favour, just as it has been since those first, evidently distressing days after the Queen's death, when with great stoicism and commitment our new King criss-crossed the country to complete a gruelling schedule of events.

"King Charles III is the oldest person to inherit the British throne and he follows his record-breaking mother, who was the longest reigning Monarch, by quite some way," says Tracy, joint Chief Curator of Historic Royal Palaces, Chief Executive of the Heritage Education Trust and a regular broadcaster, public speaker and the author of many highly acclaimed history books and a best-selling historic fiction trilogy. "The idea of anyone else taking on a huge new job at the age of 73 is unthinkable, and yet it was an incredibly smooth transition from our longest reigning Monarch.

Charles seemed immediately like a safe pair of hands and I think he has made a really strong start."

"It can go two ways, if you've had as long a training ground as Prince of Wales. Some former Princes, such as George the Prince Regent [later George IV] didn't really put that time to good use, he just used the advantage of lots of status but no responsibility. But as Prince Charles, our new King always took his role incredibly seriously.

"Throughout history, one of the key criteria for success has been when Monarchs are in tune with what matters to their people, I think that this is absolutely the case with the new King. He involved himself in a great deal of charitable work, including setting up The Prince's Trust, and stayed on top of key issues that were important to people. We have also come to realise how forward thinking he was, certainly in terms of the environment where previously, he was not taken seriously. I think that has set him in good stead."

Tracy points to the restoration of Charles II as the key event which allowed our Monarchy to thrive. At the time, Parliament invited the exiled Charles back to the throne as a constitutional, symbolic Monarch, a restriction on royal power which was made law in 1689.

"This saved the British Monarchy. It was a big concession to make, but it was pragmatic," says Tracy. "Other Monarchies in Europe laughed and they clung on to their absolutist power, but look what eventually happened to them. Our Monarchy survived, because it was no longer a threat to Parliament in the same way that others were."

Another factor for our enduring Monarchy is identified by Tracy as its chameleon-like quality. It has evolved to ▶

weather the storms of rebellion, revolution and war and continued to take a pragmatic approach in response to needs and opinions, and to be the driving force behind profound change in matters of religion, politics and culture. It has also set precedents - both good and bad - for successors.

"It hasn't been dangerously inflexible like some Monarchies, it has adapted. It is said that a good Monarch must be, 'Always changing and always the same' - it's a great upholder of tradition and pomp and pageantry and that's part of the key to the success of the Monarchy, but it has also had to adapt, to streamline, to become more cost effective. In his first speech, King Charles referred to his late mother's "abiding love of tradition but fearless embrace of progress".

Continuing the legacy

The continuity of the Monarchy was something stressed immediately after the Queen's death. The King paid homage to the 'promise of destiny kept' by his beloved mother, declaring, "That promise of lifelong service I renew to you all today. The role and the duties of Monarchy also remain, as does the Sovereign's particular relationship and responsibility towards the Church of England — the Church in which my own faith is so deeply rooted. In that faith, and the values it inspires, I have been brought up to cherish a sense of duty to others, and to hold in the greatest respect the precious traditions, freedoms and responsibilities of our unique history and our system of parliamentary government."

The King was also keen to set out the path ahead, announcing that Prince William was now created Prince of Wales, in addition to assuming his father's former role as Duke of Cornwall and his Scottish titles. The new Prince of Wales will undoubtedly play a key role as one pair of the trusted hands into which his father will deliver the charities and issues which have absorbed him for decades.

"Lord Lyndhurst, who was Lord High Chancellor for three Monarchs in the 19th century, said, "The Sovereign always exists, the person only is changed," Tracy concludes. "It reflects the idea that the Monarchy is far more than the person who wears the crown. The indications that the new King gave are that he is going to uphold that sense of tradition and continuity but of course the Monarchy is going to have to continue to adapt and move with the times, as well."

"The late Queen's reign proves that what people value is that sense of duty and constancy. In her, Charles had an incredible role model to follow. He really learned from the best."

Charles I, II and III

"Of course, parallels will be drawn between Charles III and with the previous two King Charles and there are some interesting comparisons to be made," says Tracy. "But times have changed. The throne that he has inherited is rather different to that of Charles I and II and he is being crowned in a completely different world."

"Charles III has had a very long training. It was very different for the first two Charles, although they had a decent amount of time to prepare. The parallels probably get most interesting with Charles II because when he restored the Monarchy in 1660, he came into a situation that was radically different. He came back very much on Parliament's invitation and had to accept this new world order, whereby Parliament was in charge and the Monarchy

Crown & Sceptre

Originally released ahead of the Platinum Jubilee, Tracy's re-released book *Crown & Sceptre: A New History of the British Monarchy from William the Conqueror to Charles III* is an updated appraisal and evaluation of an institution that has charted 1,150 years across a succession of 42 kings and queens, now incorporating the milestone events of last year.

Following a prelude which sets the scene for 1066, the book tracks the line of monarchs from the Normans onwards, covering all key historic events to the accession of our new king.

"It has been fascinating to get that sweep of history," says Tracy. "It was a complete journey of discovery and themes started to emerge. I worked sequentially, Monarch by Monarch, but *Crown & Sceptre* is not just a series of potted biographies, it also looks at the Monarchy as an institution and how that has changed and survived, weathering the storms of rebellion, revolution and war. The book explores what makes it unique, and what makes it durable even now, with every royal crisis." •

was largely symbolic in terms of its political power. It was really the beginning of a constitutional monarchy, which we still have today and that balance of power is still very much with Parliament. In contrast, Charles I famously rode roughshod over his Parliament and plunged the country into civil war."

"There are very different characters involved, too. Charles II is viewed as this hedonistic pleasure seeker, who put a bit of a smile back on people's faces after the austerity of the Civil War, but was criticised for his excess. But in Charles III you have a King with a very keen social conscience who has for a long time been immersed in charitable work and in environmental causes. He certainly has a much greater sense of responsibility than his ancestors."

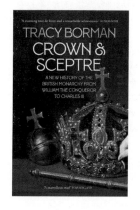

CROWN & SCEPTRE: A NEW HISTORY OF THE BRITISH MONARCHY FROM WILLIAM THE CONQUEROR TO CHARLES III BY TRACY BORMAN IS PUBLISHED BY HODDER AND STOUGHTON. THE CORONATION MONTH OF MAY ALSO MARKS THE RELEASE OF TRACY'S NEW BOOK, ANNE BOLEYN & ELIZABETH I: THE MOTHER AND DAUGHTER WHO MADE HISTORY.

The Queen's
legacy

NOTCHING UP OVER SEVEN
DECADES OF SERVICE, THE QUEEN
BECAME A GLOBAL SYMBOL OF
STABILITY AND RESILIENCE.

THE NEW MONARCH'S FIRST TROOPING OF THE COLOUR

K ing Charles follows in the footsteps of his mighty mother who celebrated her Platinum Jubilee only months before her sad passing. The only British Monarch to reign for 70 years, her legacy is an incredible milestone in history. We take a look back at the decades of her service.

The 1950's

The 19050s were a time of huge change in Britain. The decade began with the country ravaged by war and food rationing was still in force. The Coronation in 1953 heralded a feeling of optimism, a time to say goodbye to the austerity of the past and start building the future.

Once the Coronation had passed, the Queen had to look to the future, too. She was only in her mid-20s and it was time to make her mark as the Monarch. One of her first undertakings was a six-month tour of the Commonwealth, from Bermuda to Australia, the Coco Islands to Malta. Everywhere she went she was treated like a superstar, with thousands turning out to cheer her. Her final visit was to Gibraltar where she was reunited with her children and together the family sailed home in the newly launched Royal Yacht Britannia.

And so her reign began in the way it continued, visiting all the corners of her kingdom and her Commonwealth — waving, shaking hands, encouraging and being visible, never shirking her duty to her country. She met great leaders and film stars, ambassadors and politicians and treated them all the same as the countless shipbuilders, nurses, soldiers and homemakers she met on engagements around the country. ▶

THE QUEEN DURING HER VISIT TO CAIRNS, AUSTRALIA

THE FAMILY INDULGING IN ONE OF THEIR FAVOURITE ACTIVITIES

1957, THE QUEEN WITH PRESIDENT EISENHOWER, HIS WIFE AND PRINCE PHILIP BEFORE A STATE DINNER

PRINCE CHARLES' INVESTITURE IN 1969 IN WALES.

THE QUEEN'S SILVER JUBILEE

The 1960's

The decade kicked off with a double celebration for The Royal Family. The birth of Prince Andrew in February (the first child born to a reigning Monarch for over 100 years) and Princess Margaret's marriage to Anthony Armstrong-Jones at Westminster Abbey.

More firsts followed over the years... Prince Philip was the first member of The Royal Family to give a TV interview to Richard Dimbleby in 1961. The Queen's Gallery was open to display the Royal Collection in 1962, and the Queen was the first Monarch to visit Germany officially in 52 years with an 11-day tour of West Germany in 1965.

The decade was not without controversy. The Aberfan disaster, saw a landmine of coal waste crash into a small mining village killing 144, including 116 children. The Queen was criticised for waiting a full week to visit the site of the tragedy.

The decade ended with Prince Charles' investiture as Prince of Wales at Caernarfon Castle in July 1969 and an unprecedented glimpse into the lives of the Royals with the release of the documentary, 'Royal Family'. "The salad is ready," the Queen trilled as Philip manned the BBQ at a family picnic at Balmoral. Her subjects watched in wonder.

A HISTORIC MOMENT FOR THE WORLD - VISITING WEST GERMANY

QUEEN RECEIVING DIGNITARIES AT BUCKINGHAM PALACE, BEING FILMED BY THE BBC

VISITING BEIJING, CHINA

The 1970's

The 1970s was the Queen's fabulous silver decade – not only did she mark 25 years of marriage to Prince Philip in 1972, she also celebrated with her whole nation as everyone joined in to mark the milestone of the 25th anniversary of her succession to the throne.

People up and down the UK wanted to join in the celebrations and, in London alone, one million people lined the streets, many of whom had camped out overnight to secure a good vantage point. They watched The Royal Family on their way to St Paul's Cathedral to mark the start of the Queen's Silver Jubilee celebrations, the Queen resplendent in pink as she led the procession in the golden state coach. Millions more took the day off work and thousands of street parties were held to mark the occasion.

Later that same year, there was another personal cause for celebration for The Royal Family when Her Majesty and Prince Philip became grandparents for the first time when Princess Anne gave birth to her son Peter.

Politically, the Queen made history when she received the first female Prime Minister at Buckingham Palace in 1979, following a landslide victory for the Conservative Party over the presiding Labour government, which saw Margaret Thatcher voted into power.

THE CHRISTENING OF PRINCESS ANNE'S SON, PETER

THE FIRST FEMALE PRIME MINISTER

PRINCE CHARLES MARRIES LADY DIANA

The 1980's

Throughout her reign, the Queen always did her utmost to break down political barriers and build bridges with nations throughout the world, and consequently she travelled more than any sovereign in history.

1986 saw her make a momentous State visit to China – the first visit from any reigning British Monarch, and one that came after initial negotiations to return Hong Kong to China.

At the beginning of the decade, she marked a new religious milestone when, as head of the Church of England, she received Pope John Paul II at Buckingham Palace – the first visit from a Roman Catholic Pontiff in over 450 years.

The 1980s also saw the Falkland conflict – something that affected the Queen deeply as both Head of the Armed Forces and on a more personal level, as a mother – Prince Andrew was the pilot of a Sea King helicopter during the conflict. It was with much relief that the Queen met her son as he returned to Portsmouth on his ship.

The 1980s also brought the Queen great joy in the form of the wedding of her son Prince Charles to Lady Diana Spencer and four new grandchildren. Zara Phillips, Prince William, Prince Harry and Princess Beatrice. Celebrations also took place to mark her 60th birthday in London and Windsor. ▶

SANDRINGHAM IN 1988, THE QUEEN AND PRINCE PHILIP WITH THEIR GRANDCHILDREN PRINCES HARRY AND WILLIAM WITH MASTER PETER PHILLIPS AND SISTER ZARA

MEETING WITH NELSON MANDELA

The 1990's

Having seen two estrangements and one divorce in the family and suffering the calamity of Windsor Castle, her childhood home, almost burning to the ground, The Queen labelled 1992 her 'annus horribilis'.

Five years later, she bid a sad farewell to the Royal Yacht Britannia, where she had spent many happy holidays.

Much worse was to come when Diana, Princess of Wales, was killed in a horrific car crash. Her tragic loss was mourned far beyond The Royal Family.

Yet there was plenty to celebrate in the 1990s. Princess Anne found love again with Commander Timothy Laurence, marrying him in an intimate ceremony at Crathie Kirk in Scotland. Seven years later her younger brother Edward settled down with Sophie Rhys Jones.

All through those years, state matters continued apace. The Queen met Nelson Mandela both on his home pitch and on hers, and for the first time she toured former Eastern Bloc countries such as Poland and Czech Republic.

And devolution in 1999 saw the milestone openings of the National Assembly of Wales and the Parliament of Scotland. Celebrating the turn of the Millennium at London's Millennium Dome, the Queen had quite a decade to look back on and much to look forward to.

MOURNING THE LOSS OF PRINCESS DIANA

LIGHTING A BEACON FLOATING IN THE THAMES AS SHE TRAVELS BY BOAT, TO THE MILLENNIUM DOME AT GREENWICH

The 2000's

The noughties brought the Queen celebration alongside sorrow. The opening of the Millennium Dome at Greenwich kick-started the new millennium in style, followed by the opening of Tate Modern. However, personal sadness struck when the Queen lost her sister, Princess Margaret (aged 71) on February 9th following a stroke. Just weeks later on March 30, Queen Elizabeth, the Queen Mother passed away at the grand age of 101 at the Royal Lodge, Windsor. The Queen attended her funeral at Westminster Abbey before a private committal at St George's Chapel.

The Golden Jubilee of 2002 marked the 50th anniversary celebration of the Queen's accession in 1952, with the Queen being one of only a handful of British Monarchs to reach such a milestone; the last had been Queen Victoria. A massive programme of events marked the occasion, including Royal visits to Jamaica, New Zealand, Australia and Canada, a tour of the UK visiting 70 towns and cities and a national weekend of celebrations, including two concerts held in the gardens of Buckingham Palace. Then in 2003 came the arrival of Lady Louise Windsor, daughter of the Earl and Countess of Wessex, born in November.

THE DEATH OF THE BELOVED QUEEN MOTHER WAS A HARD TIME

INVESTIGATING THE FIRE
AT WINDSOR CASTLE

CELEBRATING THE
DIAMOND JUBILEE

CELEBRATING THE MARRIAGE
OF CATHERINE AND WILLIAM

THE QUEEN DURING THE
GOLDEN JUBILEE CELEBRATIONS

The 2010's-Present

An action packed couple of decades for The Royal Family. Kicking off with Prince William proposing to his sweetheart, Kate Middleton during a holiday in Kenya in 2010. Millions tuned in to watch the nuptials which took place at Westminster Abbey.

During that same year the Queen's granddaughter, Zara Phillips married former rugby player, Mike Tindall in a far lower key ceremony at Canongate Kirk in Edinburgh.

The Queen welcomed her first great-grandchild that year also, born to Peter Phillips (son of Princess Anne) and his wife, Autumn. The baby girl was named Savannah. Two years later, the couple had another daughter named Isla.

Future King, Prince George was born to Catherine and William in 2013, followed by Princess Charlotte in 2015.

Several years later Prince Harry was linked to actress, Meghan Markle after they were matched on a blind date. 16 months after meeting, the couple became engaged.

In 2018, the pair wed at St George's Chapel at Windsor Castle, in an equally high-profile celebration as that of his brother some years earlier.

Princess Eugenie also married her long-term partner in 2018. Meanwhile her sister, Beatrice became engaged.

William and Catherine welcomed Prince Louis in 2018, whilst Harry's son, Archie arrived in 2019 and his daughter Lilibet, named after his grandmother, was born in 2021.

The Queen celebrated the incredible milestone of the Platinum Jubilee in 2022. The first British Monarch to mark seven decades of service. Celebrations and events took place around the world and over a four-day bank holiday weekend in the United Kingdom.

Sadly, just a few months later, Queen Elizabeth II passed away peacefully on the 8th of September 2022 at one of her favourite places - Balmoral Castle in Scotland.

The State Funeral for Her Majesty took place at Westminster Abbey on Monday 19th September at 11am. •

THE NATION MOURNED
THE DEATH OF THE QUEEN

Following in the footsteps of previous Kings

OVER THE LAST 200 YEARS THERE HAVE BEEN SIX KINGS TO PRECEDE CHARLES III

George IV (*George Augustus Frederick*)	Reigned: 29th January 1820 – 26th June 1830 (10 years, 149 days)

When George IV's father George III became seriously ill, he ascended to the throne. George had previously acted as Prince Regent for 9 years during his father's illness, before his ascension in 1820, age 48.

As a young man, the King was considered extravagant and sociable, though perhaps too loose with his spending. He had a keen eye for art, architecture and interior design and was the patron of many artists including Thomas Gainsborough and David Wilkie. He collected a vast array of paintings, drawings and sculptures and had a particular love of French furniture.

One of George's most famous Royal residences was his seaside retreat, built for him by famed Carlton House architect, Henry Holland and also worked on by William Porden and John Nash in later years. The spectacular estate is now known as The Royal Pavilion.

As a Prince, George married twice, though his first marriage, at age 23 was deemed illegal. He had become infatuated with Maria Fitzherbert, who was Roman Catholic, after meeting her when he was just 21. Their union could not stand as it went against both the Act of Settlement 1701, due to her religion, and the Royal Marriages Act 1772 that barred heirs marrying under the age of 25 without the King's explicit consent. His second marriage was to Princess Caroline of Brunswick and the pair welcomed one child, a daughter named Charlotte, then separated shortly after.

During his reign, George IV visited Ireland, which had not been visited by a Monarch for over 70 years and Scotland which no King had visited since 1651. But he spent the latter years as King in seclusion, having lost his only child, Princess Charlotte, who died giving birth to a stillborn son. Because he had no living heirs, on his death the crown passed to his brother, Prince William.

William IV (William Henry)

Reigned: 26th June 1830 - 20th June 1837 (6 years, 360 days)

Having served in the Navy as a young man, on his ascension to the thrown, William earned the nickname 'The Sailor King'. At the age of 64, he was the eldest Prince crowned King in British History, before being surpassed by King Charles III in 2022. William IV was not only the King of Britain, but of Hanover too.

At the start of his reign, William was popular because he was seen as more down-to-earth, hard-working and frugal than his late older brother. But the Reform Crisis quickly put paid to that as the nation turned on him. On occasion he was even hissed at in public.

However, as the dust settled on the crisis, his popularity was somewhat restored, though it never reached the heights it did when he first took to the throne.

William had 11 illegitimate children during his time as a Prince, and though he wed Princess Adelaide of Saxe-Meiningen shortly before becoming King, the marriage did not produce a surviving heir. This meant upon William's death, the crown would be passed to his niece, Princess Alexandrina Victoria of Kent. But as his health deteriorated before the Princess had come of age, there was a risk her mother, the Duchess of Kent, who William disliked for slighting his wife, would become Regent.

During his final birthday gathering, he gave a speech saying, "I trust to God that my life may be spared for nine months longer... I should then have the satisfaction of leaving the exercise of the Royal authority to the personal authority of that young lady, heiress presumptive to the Crown, and not in the hands of a person now near me."

Being so public about his dislike of the Princess's mother, was shocking at the time. However, he did manage to hold on until just a month after the Princess turned 18 and on his death she became Queen Victoria, heralding in the Victorian Era for Great Britain. ►

"I trust to God that my life may be spared for nine months longer... I should then have the satisfaction of leaving the exercise of the Royal authority to the personal authority of that young lady, heiress presumptive to the Crown, and not in the hands of a person now near me."

Edward VII (Albert Edward)

Reigned: 22th January 1901 – 6th May 1910
(9 years, 105 days)

Victoria was Queen for 63 years, at the time the longest reign in British history, and was popular with the public, leaving her son, Edward VII, with some very big shoes to fill on her passing.

But Edward made the role of Sovereign his own, focussing heavily on foreign affairs as he was fluent in both French and German, and helping to repair the relationship between Britain and France. In fact he is widely considered to have been crucial in making the Anglo-French Entente Cordiale of 1904 possible.

His foreign tours helped earn favour with the public, but it was his visits around Britain, carrying out various duties, that not only helped secure his popularity, but also set the precedent for the duties and British tours carried out by The Royal Family today.

Married to Alexandra of Denmark, the couple resided between Marlborough House and Sandringham, where they loved to entertain, often throwing lavish parties. The couple were regarded as very fashionable and the King set trends with his love for tweed, Norfolk jackets and wearing black instead of white ties at dinner.

Edward VII was also an avid advocate of the arts, he helped found the Royal College of Music and introduced new honours such as the Order of Merit which recognises contributions to arts and sciences.

Towards the end of his life, he suffered repeated illnesses. At one point he had several heart attacks in a row, but refused to lie down saying, "No, I shall not give in; I shall go on; I shall work to the end."

However he died later that day age 68, and his son George V became King.

George V (George Frederick Ernest Albert) | Reigned: 6th May 1910 – 20th January 1936 (25 years, 260 days)

Ascending to the throne age 45, George's reign took place during a time of great upheaval and political change around the world. He was in power at the start of communism, fascism and socialism as well as, the Russian Revolution, Irish republicanism and the Indian independence movement.

But one of the biggest challenges of his reign was of course the start of the first World War in 1914. It was at this time that the King changed the name of the Royal House from the German sounding House of Saxe-Coburg and Gotha to the House of Windsor, which it is still known as today.

During the war, George visited the troops over 450 times and visited hospitals treating injured servicemen more than 300 times. George also started the Christmas broadcast by the reigning Monarch, in 1932.

Married to Mary of Teck, the union was a very happy one, and the pair were said to be utterly devoted to each other. Their marriage produced five children. He favoured his second son Prince Albert (who he called Bertie but would be later known as George VI) and he doted in particular on his granddaughter, Elizabeth who he affectionately nicknamed Lilibet.

As the end of his life neared, he once said, "I pray to God my eldest son will never marry and have children, and that nothing will come between Bertie and Lilibet and the throne." Which of course came to pass as both George VI and his beloved Lilibet, known as Queen Elizabeth II, both became Monarchs.

However, when George died aged 70 and was succeeded briefly by his eldest son Edward. ►

IMAGE CREDIT: SHUTTERSTOCK

Edward was a qualified pilot and undertook many Royal tours whilst his father was still alive, visiting underprivileged countries as well as areas of deprivation in Britain, which resulted in him being well-regarded by the public.

However, his private life was not so celebrated. He was known to have had affairs with married women, but shortly before becoming King, he fell head over heels in love with one married woman in particular. American socialite Wallis Simpson sought a divorce from her second husband, and it became clear that Edward intended to marry her. Advisors tried desperately to dissuade him from the union, stating it was not proper for a man of his standing in both the Monarchy and the Church of England, to wed a twice-divorced woman whose former husbands were still living.

Edward tried to find a solution, proposing he be allowed to marry Simpson but that she would not be known as Queen Consort and any children they had would not be official heirs. Though this plan garnered support in the form of Winston Churchill, it was ultimately rejected.

Edward stood firm and less than a year into his reign he abdicated the throne. He told the world via a BBC broadcast stating, "I have found it impossible to carry the heavy burden of responsibility and to discharge my duties as King as I would wish to do without the help and support of the woman I love."

The title of King was then passed to his eldest brother.

"I have found it impossible to carry the heavy burden of responsibility and to discharge my duties as king as I would wish to do without the help and support of the woman I love."

George VI
(Albert Frederick Arthur George)

Reigned: 11th December 1936 - 6th February 1952 (15 years, 58 days)

Whilst the Kings that came before him knew the Crown would be theirs, it was sudden and surprising for George VI to become the British Monarch upon his brother's abdication.

Having served in the Royal Navy and Royal Air Force during the World War I, when the second World War broke out a couple of years into his reign, he knew first-hand what the troops were going through, and made a concerted effort to visit with them whenever possible.

Throughout the war he showed solidarity with the country by staying at his home in Buckingham Palace with wife Queen Elizabeth and their two daughters. Even after the Palace was bombed nine times, he remained steadfast. This earned him huge respect from the British public who were enduring terribly dark days as the war waged on.

The King and Queen visited many bomb-sites throughout Britain, and tried fervently to boost morale in the country.

Although he lived to see the end of the Second World War it, alongside his heavy smoking, had taken a toll on his health resulting in a lung operation that he never fully recovered from. He died in his sleep at 56, passing the Crown to his eldest Daughter Elizabeth. And now, 71 years later, her son Charles is King. •

THE WORLD IN 1948

CHRISTENING DAY WITH HIS MOTHER, GRANDFATHER AND GREAT-GRANDMOTHER

The year the future King was born.

Charles was born just three years after World War 2 had ended. 1948 was a time of great change not just for the United Kingdom, but the for the whole world. Communists in Czechoslovakia, the assassination of a beloved spiritual leader, Windrush, the return of the Olympics, it was a busy year full of ups and downs. But the birth of a new Prince was a moment of joy after a very difficult few years for the world.

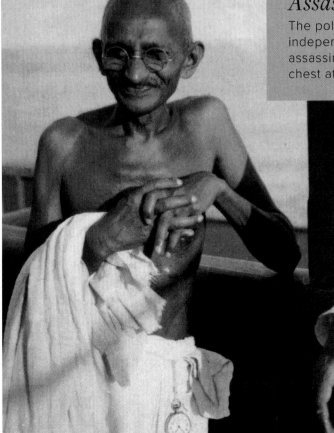

Assassination of Gandhi

The political and spiritual leader of the Indian independence movement, Mahatma Gandhi was assassinated after being shot three times in the chest at close range on 30 January 1948. ►

The World Health Organization was formed by the United Nations.

Communists seized control of Czechoslovakia.

Hells Angels, a motorcycle gang, is formed in California.

Photography advances

The first camera to produce photographs instantly, was developed by Edwin Land. It went on sale as the Polaroid Land Camera.

A Long-Standing Union

Ernest Bevin, the British Foreign Secretary, proposed to form a Western Union with France and the Benelux countries to make a stand against the Soviet Union. It became a predecessor to NATO.

The railways around Britain become nationalised and British Railways is formed.

Car Racing

A stock car racing organisation is created in the USA called NASCAR.

Windrush

A large group of Afro-Caribbean immigrants arrive in Britain on a ship named Empire Windrush.

Rudolf Dassler set up the sports shoe company Puma after a feud with his brother 'Adi' – who set up rival company Adidas.

The big screen version of Hamlet, by Laurence Olivier, debuted in London.

Return of the Olympics

The Summer Olympics kicks off in London, marking the first Summer Olympics since 1936 in Berlin

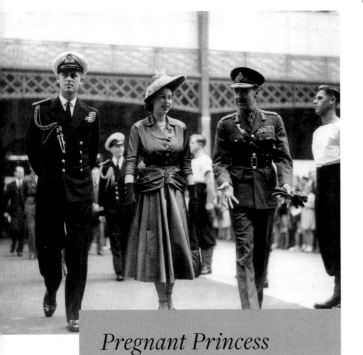

Pregnant Princess

Princess Elizabeth and husband Philip arrive at Olympia to watch The Royal Tournament. The Princess was four months pregnant with her first child, Charles.

The first ever 'monkey astronaut' Albert I, is launched into space from a New Mexico site.

The Berlin Blockade begins.

The NHS launches in the UK, providing free universal healthcare.

A sector of Alcohol Anonymous is founded in London for the first time.

Korea divides into two political entities - North Korea and South Korea.

The United Nations General Assembly adopts the Universal Declaration of Human Rights.

Other famous people born in 1948

Some other notable figures were born in this year of great change ●

Ozzy Osbourne   Stevie Nicks   Samuel L. Jackson   Olivia Newton-John

EARLY
years

BORN TO A PRINCESS WHO
BECOME QUEEN A FEW SHORT
YEARS LATER, CHARLES'
FORMATIVE YEARS WERE FULL
OF UPS AND DOWNS

J ust under a year after his parents, Princess Elizabeth and Prince Philip wed, their first child, a son they named Charles Philip Arthur George, was born. The happy couple welcomed their child, weighing seven pounds and six ounces, in the Buhl Room at Buckingham Palace on the evening of November 14th, 1948.

Princess Elizabeth, then aged 22, went through 30 hours of labour before surgeons stepped in and performed a C-section, right there in the palace.

The birth of the young Prince broke a centuries long tradition of Royal births being witnessed by a senior politician. It's believed that the tradition was introduced to ensure the new Royal baby could not be swapped at birth. However, Princess Elizabeth's father, King George VI stepped in during his daughter's labour and decreed that she did not need to follow previous protocol and could give birth privately as was her wish.

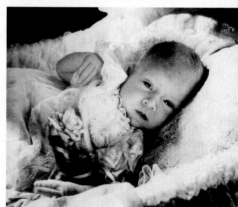

"His birth was just the first of many traditions the new heir would break over the coming years."

His birth was just the first of many traditions the new heir would break over the coming years.

His father was not present when he was born, instead he played squash to distract himself and make the time pass quicker. However, on hearing the news of his son's arrival, Prince Philip bounded up the stairs to the Buhl Room to see his beloved wife and first born, whom he described as looking rather like a "Plum Pudding." He then presented his wife with a bouquet of red roses and carnations.

The arrival of the new heir was announced by the King's Troop Royal Artillery firing a 41-gun salute and the bells of Westminster rang, which lead to crowds flocking to the palace to celebrate the happy news. A month later, Charles was christened at Buckingham Palace, by the Archbishop of Canterbury. ►

*"As a baby and toddler,
Charles spent much of his
time with his grandparents"*

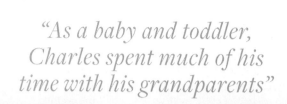

As a baby and toddler, Charles spent much of his time with his grandparents, the King and Queen, whilst his mother and father were in Malta, where Prince Philip was stationed in the Royal Navy. However, his beloved grandfather died when he was only three, changing the family's lives forever.

Overnight Princess Elizabeth became Queen and Charles became the official heir apparent. By then he had a little sister, Princess Anne, with whom he spent much of his time when his parents were away on official duty, completing long overseas tours.

Indeed he also grew very close to his grandmother, the Queen Mother, during those years and credits her with introducing him to the world of music and art. "My grandmother was the person who taught me to look at things." Charles said, many years later, going on to describe her as, "The most magical grandmother you could possibly have."

When the time came to begin his education, Charles was first home-schooled by Catherine Peebles, his Glaswegian governess. However, by the age of eight, his parents felt he would benefit from being surrounded by other children in a classroom. And so came the time for Prince Charles to break another Royal tradition, he became the first ever heir to the throne to attend school when he was sent to Cheam, a boarding school in Hampshire.

His secondary education saw him sent to Gordonstoun in Scotland, the same boarding school his father had attended. Unfortunately, Prince Charles describes the day his father flew him to an old RAF base, before driving him the rest of the way to the school, to be the start of his "prison sentence". Each day at school would begin with a run, often in extreme weather, followed by a freezing cold shower.

There has also been talk of a culture of bullying, from which the young prince was not exempt. Since a Prince was attending the school, many of the rules became even stricter than before, and his fellow students often took it out on Charles. One of his schoolmates describes Charles' time there as, "crushingly lonely" since most of the other children avoided the young Prince and anyone who did try to make friends with him found themselves taunted with constant 'slurping' sounds to indicate that they were sucking up to him. ►

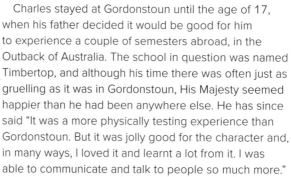

Charles stayed at Gordonstoun until the age of 17, when his father decided it would be good for him to experience a couple of semesters abroad, in the Outback of Australia. The school in question was named Timbertop, and although his time there was often just as gruelling as it was in Gordonstoun, His Majesty seemed happier than he had been anywhere else. He has since said "It was a more physically testing experience than Gordonstoun. But it was jolly good for the character and, in many ways, I loved it and learnt a lot from it. I was able to communicate and talk to people so much more."

Indeed, Charles found the other students in his new school to be far more accepting of him and his status as heir to the British throne, which he had previously found himself isolated for at his former schools.

When he returned from Australia, Charles was far more confident and relaxed than he had been just six months prior and so he found his final year of education back in Gordonstoun a lot more bearable than previous years.

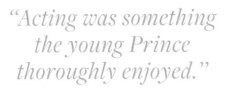

"Acting was something the young Prince thoroughly enjoyed."

Upon graduating Gordonstoun, Charles broke tradition for the third time, choosing to go straight to university rather than enrol in the British Armed Forces and was the first heir to receive a university degree. Charles attended Trinity College at Cambridge where he studied anthropology, history and archaeology.

During his time at university, Charles joined the Dryden Society, a popular drama club that saw him take part in plays and sketches – acting was something the young Prince thoroughly enjoyed.

When he was 20, Charles formerly became Prince of Wales. The investiture, which saw his mother officially crown him as the Prince of Wales, was watched by 500 million people around the world.

A year later, Charles went on to obtain a 2:2 degree from Cambridge, and it was on his graduation that his real life as the heir apparent truly began. •

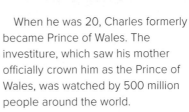

The world's most
ELIGIBLE BACHELOR

Since Charles was just three years old, he has been heir apparent. Unlike his mother, who was thrust into the position of heir and then Queen, quickly and without prior warning, Charles has known since he was a toddler that he would be King. And so has the world. So perhaps it's not that surprising that once he came of age, he was officially thought of as the most eligible bachelor in the world.

With the bright blue eyes of his mother and the noble height of his father, he was a fine figure of a man. So it was almost a given that the dashing Prince became quite the pin up. And by his 20th birthday, the questions about when he would choose a bride had already begun.

In his one of his first televised interviews, he was asked by a reporter, "Do you have any thoughts about the lady that a Prince of Wales should marry?" The young Prince appeared visibly shy in the face of such a question. Although he did let out a small laugh before replying, "You have got to remember that when you marry in my position, you are going to marry somebody who perhaps one day is going to become a Queen, and you have got to choose somebody very carefully."

Of course, being heir to the British throne brings with it a substantial amount of pressure, as he touched upon in that very interview. But his 20s was not dedicated to finding a wife, in fact his great uncle, Lord Mountbatten, took him under his wing and actively encouraged the bachelor Prince to enjoy his youth and have many dates before settling down.

Following this advice, young Charles stepped out from the shadow of his parents and saw his confidence ►

THE YOUNG PRINCE AFTER A FALL AT A POLO MATCH IN 1972

'It's no surprise the dashing prince became quite the pin up.'

increase tenfold as he was suddenly presented as somewhat of a playboy in the press. He had a debonair charm that drew those he met to him, and women the world over swooned at the handsome bachelor who would one day be King.

It helped that he became thought of as an action man, with his time in the military and the many photographs of him skiing and of course excelling at polo, only adding to his allure. It was during this time in the 70s, that Charles was linked to a whole host of beautiful women, whom the press at the time dubbed 'Charlie's Angels.'

But after 10 or so years, his bachelor days came to an end with his marriage to the young Lady Diana Spencer, a marriage that although ill-fated, did of course go on to produce two wonderful sons in Princes Harry and William.

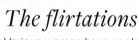

THE PRINCE AT A BASKETBALL
GAME WITH TRICIA NIXON IN 1970

The flirtations

Various women have spoken very fondly of Charles over the years, but the exact nature of their relationships has never been confirmed.

ACTRESS JANE PRIEST AMBUSHES
CHARLES WITH A KISS IN AUSTRALIA 1979

WITH SHIRLEY BASSEY AT A
CONCERT IN WALES IN 1978

Charlie's Angels

These are just a few of the women who made an impact on Charles' life during his bachelor years, before he went on to wed.

Lucia Santa Cruz

Generally considered to be Charles' first proper girlfriend, she was the daughter of the Chilean ambassador.

Lady Jane Wellesley

The daughter of the 8th Duke of Wellington is said to have found the media speculation around their relationship too difficult.

Lady Amanda Knatchbull

The Prince was so smitten with Lady Amanda that he proposed to her, but the relationship didn't work out.

Davina Sheffield

The granddaughter of prominent industrialist, Lord McGowan.

Sabrina Guinness

The heir to the brewing and banking dynasty, was the IT girl of her generation for a time.

Camilla Shand

Having dated for a time in the 70s, we now know Camilla and Charles finally wed in 2005.

Anna Wallace

The daughter of a prolific Scottish landowner, Anna was said to have been Charles' last girlfriend before meeting Lady Diana.

Lady Diana Spencer

Charles and Princess Diana were married from 1981 until 1996. •

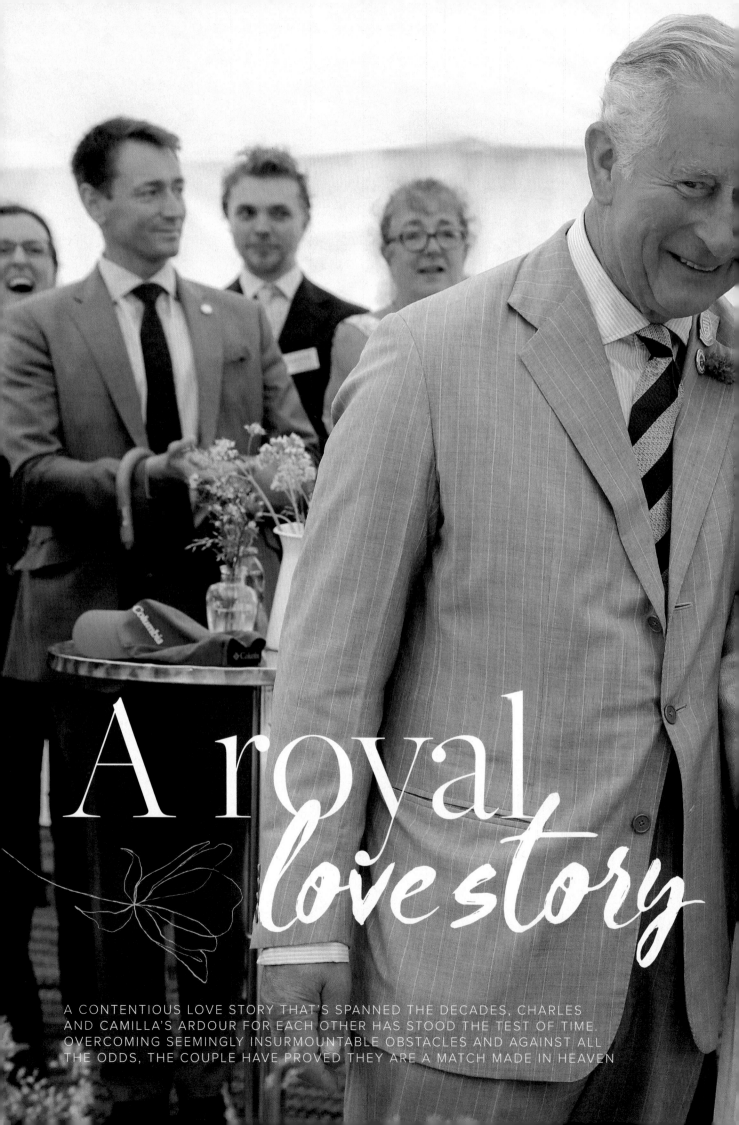

A royal
lovestory

A CONTENTIOUS LOVE STORY THAT'S SPANNED THE DECADES, CHARLES AND CAMILLA'S ARDOUR FOR EACH OTHER HAS STOOD THE TEST OF TIME. OVERCOMING SEEMINGLY INSURMOUNTABLE OBSTACLES AND AGAINST ALL THE ODDS, THE COUPLE HAVE PROVED THEY ARE A MATCH MADE IN HEAVEN

T he decades long romance has seen the couple weather both public disdain and adoration, yet despite the trials and tribulations, the love story of Charles and Camilla has stood the test of time.

Fiercely protective of their privacy, the media shy couple have regularly faced a negative barrage of public opinion, and as such rarely talk about their relationship publicly. But every so often, they cannot help but reveal their adoration for each other.

Their nervousness is understandable, after all through the 'Diana years' their popularity plummeted to an all-time low.

Whilst the couple were reported to have met in the 1970s at a polo match, their paths were already inextricably linked. The great grandmother of Camilla was said to be the mistress of the then King at the time – Charles' great grandfather. Something that Camilla apparently made a spirited reference to when the couple met again at a party.

"His destiny will come, he's always known it's going to come, and I don't think it does weigh on his shoulders at all."

The couple began dating, however when Charles returned to his post with the Navy in February 1973, it seemed that the romance was not on secure ground. The notion was solidified when Camilla rekindled a romance with a former boyfriend, Andrew Parker Bowles, who she went on to marry in the summer of that year. The marriage caused a huge amount of public interest as Andrew had also previously dated Charles' sister, Princess Anne.

Later that same decade, Charles met Diana for the first time. After briefly dating her sister Lady Sarah Spencer. Speaking on her engagement Diana revealed how she first met Prince Charles. "It was 1977, Charles came to stay. He was a friend of my sister Sarah's. [He came] for a [hunting] shoot. We sort of met in a ploughed field."

But it was 1981 before the couple announced their engagement and were married later that year. Diana was just 20 years old.

Even from the start there were concerns that Charles had selected his young bride for her suitability rather than his love for her. When asked whether they were madly in love after their engagement, he remarked. "Whatever love is."

She revealed to Andrew Morton that even during her wedding, she had Camilla on her mind. "I knew she was in there, of course. I looked for her. So walking down the aisle, I spotted Camilla, pale grey, veiled pillbox hat."

In the now notorious *Panorama* interview, Diana said. "There were three of us in the marriage, so it was a little crowded."

In the early 90s a taped phone call was released that confirmed Charles and Camilla's affair and their popularity plummeted. Meanwhile Diana's soared to epic proportions.

In the mid-90s both marriages ended in divorce. During this time Charles commented that Camilla was "a great friend of mine".

It's believed that aides were hoping to introduce her to the public gently with a view to her becoming accepted at Charles' companion, however the death of Diana in 1997 delayed that. ►

Once again the tide of negativity turned on the Royal Family, and the public were incandescent that initially there were no plans for Diana to be given a state funeral. It quickly became apparent that the nation's sweetheart must be given the send off the public believed she deserved, or The Royal Family would face one of their lowest ratings in public opinion. Plans were quickly adapted to ensure Diana was treated as a Royal and her funeral caused mourning around the globe, with millions watching the ceremony on television.

Prince Harry later revealed to Oprah the detrimental effect the funeral had on him. He said. "When my mum was taken away from me at the age of 12, just before my 13th birthday, I didn't want the [Royal] life. Sharing the grief of my mother's death with the world."

"For me, the thing I remember the most was the sound of the horses' hooves going along the pavement. Along the Mall, the red brick road. By this point I was, both of us were in shock. It was like I was outside of my body and just walking along doing what was expected of me.

"Showing one tenth of the emotion that everybody else was showing. I thought, 'This is my mum. You never even met her.'"

It's said that it was the following year before William met Camilla with Harry meeting her soon after. Charles' parents were said to be unimpressed with his choice of companion and avoided spending any time in Camilla's company. It was the very end of the 90s before Charles and Camilla were seen in public together.

IMAGE CREDIT: SHUTTERSTOCK

"You can imagine it is a real, real challenge. But she's, I think, been brilliant in the way she's tackled these things."

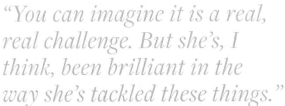

It was the turn of the century before the Queen agreed to meet Camilla as her son's partner and in 2005 the couple decided to marry. The low key ceremony took place at Windsor Guildhall.

And since then Camilla has slowly earned the respect of not only the public, but also her Royal peers. She has proven herself to be dedicated and hard-working. One of her biggest fans and appreciators is of course Charles himself. He commented "You can imagine it is a real, real challenge. But she has, I think, been brilliant in the way she's tackled these things,"

"It's always marvellous to have somebody who, you know, you feel understands and wants to encourage. Although she certainly pokes fun if I get too serious about things. And all that helps," he said. Charles and Camilla have been through a lot, and all in the public eye, but it's nice to see they have got each other's backs and still have time to share the sweet moments in life!

Camilla has remained very stoic yet supportive in her comments about the King and said previously, "His destiny will come, he's always known it's going to come, and I don't think it does weigh on his shoulders at all," she revealed in a 2018 documentary.●

Charles:
THE FAMILY MAN

As heir to the British throne, Charles always knew that he would be required to in turn produce his own heirs when the time came. But it wasn't just duty that led him to have children, indeed being a father is something he is understood to have always wanted.

He was 33 when his first child was born. He and Princess Diana welcomed son William Arthur Philip Louis on the 21st June, 1982.

Charles and Diana doted on their son, and even broke with previous Royal tradition by taking then nine-month-old William along with them on their tour of Australia and New Zealand. In the past, Royal babies had stayed at home with nannies whilst their parents carried out overseas engagements.

Two years later, the family became complete with the arrival of a second son. Prince Henry Charles Albert David (known as Prince Harry) was born on the 15th of September, 1984. He too accompanied his parents on a foreign tour as an infant, this time to Italy in 1985.

By 1996, Charles and Diana had divorced and the Princess was tragically killed in a car crash in Paris just one year later. Charles became a single father to a 12 and 15-year-old. Of that difficult time, Prince Harry spoke about his father trying to support he and his brother, "[Our father] was there for us - he was the one out of two left, and he tried to do his best and to make sure that we were protected and looked after. But he was going through the same grieving process as well."

In his controversial book, *Spare*, Harry shared more detail about what Charles was like as a father to him at that time. He wrote, "Evenings, I'd shout downstairs: 'Going to bed, Pa!' He'd always shout back cheerfully: 'I'll be there shortly, darling boy!' True to his word, minutes later he'd be sitting on the edge of my bed. He never forgot that I didn't like the dark, so he'd gently tickle my face until I fell asleep. I have the fondest memories of his hands on my cheeks, my forehead, then waking to find him gone, magically, the door always considerately left open a crack."

Charles and his boys had rather a lot of fun together, from wonderful skiing trips and partaking in countryside pursuits, to the laughs they shared during official tours and engagements.

As the years rolled by and his children grew into men, they would often go stretches of time apart from each other, with Harry spending time in the military and William at University in St Andrews and the Armed Forces. However, the bond between father and sons endured.

But it wasn't just his boys' busy lives that made being together often more difficult, as the Prince of Wales, Charles of course had a jam-packed work schedule.

Like his mother before him, King Charles takes his duty very seriously. In fact in 2019 he was voted the hardest working Royal, having carried out 521 engagements in just one year.

Prince William has talked in the past about his admiration for his father and his work ethic. "He has amazing personal discipline. He has – and it's frustrated me in the past a lot – he has a routine. The only way to fit all this stuff in is things have to be compartmentalised. The man never stops." He said.

William was of course the first to make Charles III a grandfather, with the birth of little Prince George in 2013. Speaking of the momentous occasion, Charles said at the time, "Grandparenthood is a unique moment in anyone's life, as countless kind people have told me in recent months, so I am enormously proud and happy to be a grandfather for the first time and we are eagerly looking forward to seeing the baby in the near future."

Though King Charles clearly loves his sons very much, it's well-known that he had also hoped to have a daughter one day. Perhaps that is one of the reasons Charles, known to be a kind man, was quick to step in and help when Prince Harry's then fiancé, Meghan Markle, realised her own father would not be able to attend their wedding.

When Harry asked if his father would perhaps walk his bride-to-be down the aisle on their big day, Charles was honoured. Describing the moment, Harry said in a 2018 BBC documentary, "I asked him to and I think he knew it was coming, and he immediately said, 'Yes, of course, I'll do whatever Meghan needs and I'm here to support you.' For him that's a fantastic opportunity to step up and be that support, and you know he's our father so of course he's going to be there for us."

Whilst now the relationship between Harry and his father is strained, both parties hope that one day, Charles and his boys can be as close, if not closer, than they ever have been. ▶

Sports Day Dad

Charles is seen joyfully competing at his then 7-year-old son William's school sports day alongside the other dads. He has always been fit and active, which are traits his sons have both inherited.

Father and sons Christmas cards

Here we see heartwarming Christmas cards of the now King with his children. The above was sent out in December 1994 whilst the humorous image below went out in 1995.

Time in the countryside

Charles and his boys spent a lot of time in the countryside, particularly in Scotland, when they were young. There they had the freedom and space to enjoy the great outdoors and all it had to offer with their dad.

Fun Family Holidays

Both William and Harry, along with their father, have a love for skiing and as youngsters enjoyed many trips to Klosters in Switzerland where they always looked happier than ever. That's not to say they didn't enjoy a little time in the sunshine too. Below we see Charles with Harry on his back in the sea on vacation.

SWIMMING WITH PRINCE HARRY

Hoping he and Harry can heal

The father and son, no matter what, still clearly have a lot of love for each other. Above we see Charles walk Meghan down the aisle and right we see father and son share a tender moment together.

The new heir apparent

Charles is in the unique position of knowing firsthand the pressure Prince William and Catherine are under now that he is King. ●

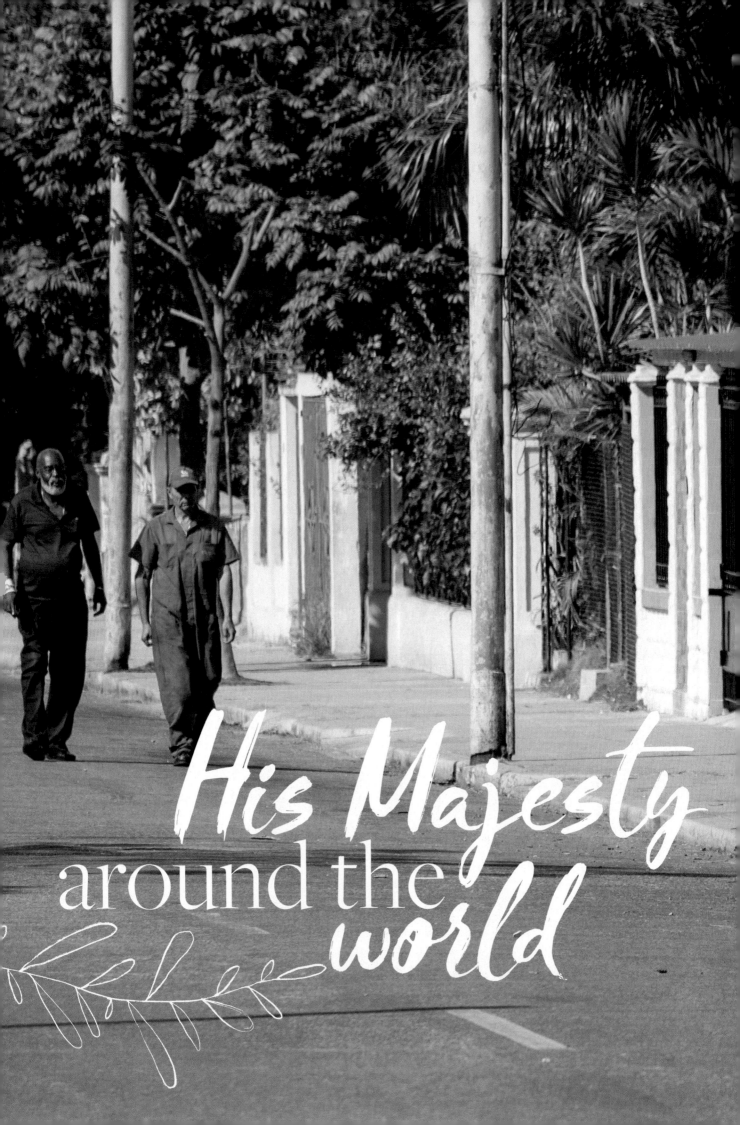

His Majesty
around the world

PRINCESS DIANA AND PRINCE CHARLES AT AYERS ROCK

RECEIVING A HONGI FROM A KUIA IN NEW ZEALAND, 2019

Australia and New Zealand

King Charles has a long-standing fondness for Australia, having of course spent time there as a teen in 1966, as a much-needed respite from his Scottish boarding school. He returned the following year, representing his late mother, Queen Elizabeth II, at the memorial service of Prime Minister Harold Holt. During the 70s, Charles went on to visit Australia a further five times, both with his mother and alone. The 80's saw him take part in a family tour, accompanied by then wife Princess Diana and his new baby boy, Prince William.

Charles has since visited Australia in particular many more times, and has often spoken of his love for the country. Shortly after the devastating floods in early 2022, Charles said, "My great admiration for the resilience, courage and compassion of the Australian people in moments like these knows no bounds."

As for New Zealand, the British Royal Family have been visiting since Prince Alfred first set foot in the country in 1869. Since then there have been over 50 Royal visits, with Charles first visiting in 1970, whilst accompanying his parents and sister, Princess Anne. Most recently he enjoyed an 8-day tour of the country with wife Camilla.

THE COUPLE IN NEW ZEALAND IN 2019

WITH PRINCESS ANNE, TRICIA NIXON AND JULIE EISENHOWER

CHARLES AND DIANA WITH GEORGE H. W. BUSH AND WIFE, BARBARA

IN PHILADELPHIA, 2007

America

The King first visited the USA in the 70s, accompanied by his sister Princess Anne when he was just 21 and one of the most eligible bachelors in the world. Perhaps it is then no surprise that the President at the time, Richard Nixon, was said to be keen the young heir apparent spend some time with his beautiful daughter Tricia. Reflecting on that visit to America Charles says, "That was quite amusing, I must say. That was the time when they were trying to marry me off to Tricia Nixon."

That pairing was of course not to be as Charles went on to marry Diana who escorted him on a visit to the Americas in 1985, which caused so much excitement that the press announced the USA had been 'Hit by a Royal Fever.'

The King has enjoyed various tours of America, his most recent in 2018 with wife Camilla by his side where he represented his mother, Queen Elizabeth II, at the funeral of President George H. W. Bush. ►

AT THE COMMON GOOD CITY FARM IN WASHINGTON

MEETING WITH PRESIDENT OBAMA AT THE WHITE HOUSE IN 2015

Caribbean

His Royal Highness has visited the Caribbean a number of times over the years, having toured Bermuda, Trinidad and Tobago, Jamaica, Antigua, Barbuda, Montserrat, St Kitts and Barbados. It was King Charles' visit to Barbados in 2021 that garnered much interest, for he was invited to the ceremony declaring the country's independence as a republic.

Whilst then still the Prince Of Wales, Charles was invited as a special Guest of Honour at the celebrations wherein the country separated itself from the British Crown. However, the Prime Minister of Barbados at the time, Mia Mottley, explained she wanted Charles there as the future Head of the Commonwealth, which Barbados has remained a part of.

PRESIDENT SANDRA MASON, AWARDS PRINCE CHARLES WITH THE ORDER OF FREEDOM OF BARBADOS

AT THE NATIONAL TRUST FOR THE CAYMAN ISLANDS' BLUE IGUANA RECOVERY CENTRE

WITH MASQUERADE DANCERS IN TRINIDAD

THE KING AND QUEEN CONSORT IN THE CAYMEN ISLANDS

WITH INGRID THOMPSON AT THE NATIONAL ARCHIVES IN BRIDGETOWN, BARBADOS

CHARLES AND CAMILLA LEAVING BAHRAIN IN 2016

THE COUPLE IN JORDAN

RIDING IN A DUNE BUGGY DURING A VISIT TO BU TINAH ISLAND

AT THE PYRAMIDS OF GIZA, EGYPT IN 2021

The Gulf and Middle East

For the first Royal tour post the Coronovirus pandemic, Charles and Camila visited The Gulf. They started in Jordan, celebrating the country's centenary, a country Charles cares for immensely, as he explained, "The Kingdom and people of Jordan have always been very dear to my heart and I have so many cherished visits over the years."

During the tour the couple also visited Egypt, where Charles spoke about the magnificent pyramids; "It defies the imagination to consider how your ancestors, with rudimentary tools, were able to construct such massive and magnificent edifices and align them almost perfectly North to South."

Whilst in Egypt he also took the opportunity to speak about the cause closest to his heart — climate change. He vowed to the people of Egypt that the UK would, "be with Egypt as your friend and partner in this epic struggle to protect and restore our environment, and to build a better future for us all."

Charles has toured much of the Middle East over the years to promote, not just environmental initiatives, but also tolerance between religious views and job opportunities for young people. ►

VISITING INDIA IN 1980

A WREATH LAYING CEREMONY AT THE ALL INDIA WAR MEMORIAL, THE INDIA GATE IN NEW DELHI

THE COUPLE ADMIRING SCULPTURES

India

Charles has visited India over 10 times and before ascending to the throne, he was the fourth Prince of Wales to tour the country. Since his first visit in 1975, His Royal Highness has always made it a priority to promote and, "to celebrate British-Indian connections." During one of his visits he was in such awe of the Taj Mahal that he vowed to one day bring his wife there. And he kept his word, touring with Camilla in recent years.

AT THE KERALA FOLKLORE THEATRE AND MUSEUM IN KOCHI, 2013

WITH QUEEN LETIZIA OF SPAIN

WITH PRINCE HARRY IN KLOSTERS, SWITZERLAND IN 1999

WITH HIS FAMILY AND KING JUAN CARLOS OF SPAIN IN MAJORCA

Europe

Whilst the King has enjoyed many tours of far-flung destinations, he has also spent many years enjoying all that his neighbouring counties in Europe have to offer. Switzerland, more specifically the Swiss Alps region, is a particular favourite of his Majesty. Charles, an avid skier, frequented the Alps many times over the years, often with his two boys in tow. However, tragedy struck in 1988 when Charles and five others were hit by an avalanche whilst skiing, and the King's friend, Major Hugh Lindsay, sadly perished. ▶

WITH THE BRITISH ARMY IN GERMANY, 1987

WALKING IN HUNGARY IN 2018

WITH PRINCESS DIANA ON
THEIR TOUR OF CANADA, 1983

CHARLES AND HIS SONS ARE
PRESENTED WITH BASEBALL JACKETS

Canada

Charles' first official tour of Canada took
place in 1970, and over the following 30
years to 2000, he returned on 12 different
occasions. He visited the country with his
first wife, Princess Diana and took along their
two children, Princes William and Harry.

In later years, Charles visited the country
with Camilla, their most recent being in 2022
as part of his mother's Jubilee celebrations.

VISITING AT RANGER
STATION AT FRED HENNE
PARK IN YELLOWKNIFE

IN A CARRIAGE AT THE
CANADA 150 CELEBRATIONS

GREETING CROWDS ON
PARLIAMENT HILL IN OTTAWA

WITH PRINCE HARRY AT THE ZULU VILLAGE OF DUKUDUKU IN NATA PROVINCE, SOUTH AFRICA

WITH NELSON MANDELA WITH THE SPICE GIRLS IN JOHANNESBURG, 1997

PLAYING A STEEL DRUM IN TRINIDAD

RECEIVING A GIFT IN KILIMANJARO IN TANZANIA

Africa

The King has undertaken a number of tours in Africa over the last 40 or so years, often taking the opportunity to talk about both sustainability and climate change. Speaking during a visit to Accra he said, "In such an uncertain and changing world, none of us can know what kind of a planet our grandchildren, and great-grandchildren, will inhabit, but the Commonwealth... offers us a vital mechanism to help ensure that it is not poisoned and polluted and that its vitality is not compromised." In 2018, during another visit to Ghana, his Majesty was made a Companion of the Order of the Star by the President, Nana Akufo-Addo. ●

ON A TOUR OF GHANA IN 2018

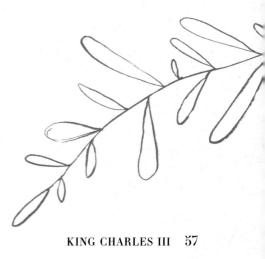

Era-defining *moments*

WE TAKE A LOOK AT SOME OF THE TIMES IT BECAME CLEAR THAT
CHARLES DISPLAYED THE METTLE HIS MOTHER WAS FAMOUS FOR

From childhood memories in Australia to family tragedy, it's the unique experiences – and hardships – that have shaped our new King. Often depicted as a somewhat reluctant Royal, there are many memorable moments where King Charles III has proved that he's more than capable of stepping into the shoes of his mighty mother.

The Investiture of HRH The Prince of Wales

On the first day of July in 1969 the Queen invested Charles as the Prince of Wales and Earl of Chester. The event took place at Caernarfon Castle in North Wales and saw the then Secretary of Wales read aloud the letters patent, issued by the Monarch granting an office or title to a person.

The Queen then gifted Charles several pieces of insignia, including a mantle, ring and sword. After which, Charles took an oath. "I, Charles, Prince of Wales, do become your liege man of life and limb and of earthly worship and faith and truth I will bear unto thee to live and die against all manner of folks.

"It is with a certain sense of pride and emotion that I have received these symbols of office, here in this magnificent fortress, where no-one could fail to be stirred by its atmosphere of time-worn grandeur, nor where I myself could be unaware of the long history of Wales in its determination to remain individual and to guard its own particular heritage,". He continued.

"One thing I am clear about and it is that Wales needs to look forward without forsaking the traditions and essential aspects of her past. The past can be just as much a stimulus to the future as anything else. By the affirmation of your loyalty today for which I express my gratitude, this will not simply be a faint hope."

Post event he said this. "Well I feel that it is a very impressive ceremony. I know perhaps some people would think it is rather anachronistic and out of place in this world, which is perhaps somewhat cynical, but I think it can mean quite a lot if one goes about it in the right way; I think it can have some form of symbolism,".

"For me, it's a way of officially dedicating one's life or part of one's life to Wales, and the Welsh people after all wanted it, and I think also the British on the whole tend to do these sorts of ceremonies rather well, and for this reason, it's done well, in fact, and I think it's been very impressive, and I hope other people thought so as well."

The Prince's Trust

Despite not yet taking the title of Monarch at the time, and after completing his duty in the Royal Navy, Charles had the incredible brainwave in 1976 to set up the Prince's Trust. Funded personally, he was dedicated to improving the lives of disadvantaged young people in the UK.

The 70s saw a time of increased unemployment and inflation which had a devastating affect on young people. Using his severance pay from the navy, a paltry £7,400, he managed to set up over 20 pilot community projects around the UK.

The following decade the charity launched the Enterprise programme which helped around one thousand young people set up their own business in just three years.

In 2016, the charity celebrated its fourth decade and to date it has helped over 1 million people. ▶

Displaying forgiveness

The Royal family retain a neutral stance when it comes to many controversial topics, but one such topic was too close to the heart of the then Prince of Wales not to speak out. Over 40 years ago King Charles lost one of his greatest confidantes, Lord Louis Mountbatten. An uncle to Prince Phillip and former Admiral of the Fleet, Lord Mountbatten was executed by the IRA, along with family members and those who worked on the boat.

More recently Charles returned to the scene and spoke of how we must move on from such tragedies.

"Through this dreadful experience, though, I now understand in a profound way the agonies borne by so many others in these islands, of whatever faith, denomination or political tradition."

Addressing the past turbulent history between Britain and Ireland, he said : "We need no longer be victims of our difficult history with each other. Without glossing over the pain of the past, we can, I believe, integrate our history and memory in order to reap their subtle harvest of possibility. Imagination, after all, is the mother of possibility. Let us, then, endeavour to become the subjects of our history and not its prisoners."

> *"Through this dreadful experience, though, I now understand in a profound way the agonies borne by so many others in these islands, of whatever faith, denomination or political tradition."*

The engagement interview

An era defining moment, though not necessarily in a positive respect, was the interview post engagement to Diana. Charles was asked the very basic question of do you love Diana and he responded with, 'whatever love means'. From that point, the British public were unsure just how perfect the relationship was. Diana later admitted that comment left her 'traumatised'. which caused a lot of people to scratch their heads.

Transparency on the end of his marriage

In 1994, the then Prince Charles gave one of his most notorious interviews. During difficult questioning by the interviewer, Jonathan Dimbleby, he was asked if he was "faithful and honourable" to his wife. He responded "Yes, absolutely." Pressed again, Charles admitted, "Until it became irretrievably broken down, us both having tried."

The small comment caused uproar and little was done to revive his public persona when he went on to refer to Camilla Parker Bowles as a 'great friend'. The then Prince alluded to that whilst he was not at that point considering divorce, he didn't consider it to be a barrier to becoming King. Although the topic was controversial, it marks a significant moment in history.

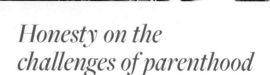

Honesty on the challenges of parenthood

Well documented as a family man, King Charles has had a turbulent life personally, but his dedication to his sons has been unwavering. He spoke honestly about being a father. "'You can attempt to impose rules and regulations, but those don't always work.

"I try to pull their legs before they pull mine off by the roots, I'm a great believer in teasing. But there's also a position you try to hold.

"You have to be very careful, I don't think you want to be best friends with your children. It's more about striking a subtle balance." ►

"You have to be very careful, I don't think you want to be best friends with your children. It's more about striking a subtle balance."

Endorsement from the highest power

After the death of the Queen, the now King Charles III gave a heartfelt speech. After which the Royal Family's official Instagram account released a quote from the Queen where she spoke of placing faith in her heir. "For Prince Philip and me, there can be no greater pleasure or comfort than to know that into his care are safely-entrusted the guiding principles of public service and duty to others," the quote read.

The caption added: "His Majesty The King has spent his working life serving the public through his patronages, with a particular focus on environmental causes and young people. His many duties in support of The Queen have included representing Her Majesty and the UK overseas, attending events including State Visits to the UK, the State Opening of Parliament and Commonwealth Heads of Government Meetings."

On the impact of Diana's death

Approaching what would have been Diana's 40th birthday, the then Prince Charles spoke candidly about the effect of her death on his sons.

"The truth is that the children mind about the way in which she is dealt with.

"It must be quite difficult for them, I think. I wish people could just let her soul rest in peace without all these constant reminders."

The Queen's Platinum Jubilee

The then HRH The Prince of Wales gave a rousing speech in tribute to the lady her referred to as 'Your Majesty, Mummy', during the Platinum Jubilee celebrations. The now King, spoke rousingly, uniting the audience in both pride and patriotism.

He said. "The scale of this evening's celebration – and the outpouring of warmth and affection over this whole Jubilee weekend – is our way of saying thank you – thank you from your family, the country, the Commonwealth, in fact the whole world.

"On behalf of us all, I wanted to pay my own tribute to your lifetime of selfless service in pictures, in words and in light.

"Your family now spans four generations. You are our Head of State. And you are also our mother.

"Your 'strength and stay' is much missed this evening but I am sure he is here in spirit... My Papa would have enjoyed the show and joined us wholeheartedly in celebrating all you continue to do for your country and your people.

"Looking back, we think of the countless State occasions that are milestones along this nation's road. And you will think of red boxes, filled with Government papers, at the end of the day.

"You will remember those who have led this country. Indeed, all the countries you serve. And leaders across the entire world.

"How things have changed... We think of all you have done to make the Commonwealth such an important force for good. You continue to make history.

"And there was still time for fun amongst the work. We might have been celebrating that Derby winner this evening... next year perhaps? But I know what really gets my mother up in the morning is all of you, Ladies and Gentlemen – all of you watching at home. Represented here tonight in this great audience.

"Your Majesty, you have been with us in our difficult times. And you bring us together to celebrate moments of pride, joy and happiness.

"You have met us and talked with us. You laugh and cry with us and, most importantly, you have been there for us, for these 70 years. You pledged to serve your whole life - you continue to deliver. That is why we are here. That is what we celebrate tonight. These pictures on your house are the story of your life – and ours. So, Your Majesty, that is why we all say "thank you".

"Ladies and Gentlemen, I know The Queen is watching these celebrations with much emotion, having, I hope, finished her marmalade sandwich, including immense regret that she cannot be here in person with us this evening. But Windsor Castle is barely 20 miles away. If we cheer loudly enough, she might, might just hear us - so let's all join together with three enormous cheers for Her Majesty!" ▶

After the death of the beloved Queen Elizabeth II

When the Queen passed away at the grand age of 96, King Charles delivered a heartfelt and uniting speech to the nation. Here is the address in full.

"I speak to you today with feelings of profound sorrow. Throughout her life, Her Majesty The Queen – my beloved mother – was an inspiration and example to me and to all my family, and we owe her the most heartfelt debt any family can owe to their mother; for her love, affection, guidance, understanding and example. Queen Elizabeth was a life well lived; a promise with destiny kept and she is mourned most deeply in her passing. That promise of lifelong service I renew to you all today.

"Alongside the personal grief that all my family are feeling, we also share with so many of you in the United Kingdom, in all the countries where the Queen was Head of State, in the Commonwealth and across the world, a deep sense of gratitude for the more than 70 years in which my mother, as Queen, served the people of so many nations.

"In 1947, on her 21st birthday, she pledged in a broadcast from Cape Town to the Commonwealth to devote her life, whether it be short or long, to the service of her peoples. That was more than a promise; it was a profound personal commitment which defined her whole life. She made sacrifices for duty. Her dedication and devotion as Sovereign never wavered, through times of change and progress, through times of joy and celebration, and through times of sadness and loss.

"As the Queen herself did with such unswerving devotion, I too now solemnly pledge myself, throughout the remaining time God grants me, to uphold the constitutional principles at the heart of our nation. And wherever you may live in the United Kingdom, or in the realms and territories across the world, and whatever may be your background or beliefs, I shall endeavour to serve you with loyalty, respect and love, as I have throughout my life.

"My life will of course change as I take up my new responsibilities. It will no longer be possible for me to give so much of my time and energies to the charities and issues for which I care so deeply. But I know this important work will go on in the trusted hands of others.

"This is also a time of change for my family. I count on the loving help of my darling wife, Camilla. In recognition of her own loyal public service since our marriage 17 years ago, she becomes my Queen Consort. I know she will bring to the demands of her new role the steadfast devotion to duty on which I have come to rely so much.

"As my heir, William now assumes the Scottish titles which have meant so much to me. He succeeds me as Duke of Cornwall and takes on the responsibilities for the Duchy of Cornwall, which I have undertaken for more than five decades. Today, I am proud to create him Prince of Wales, Tywysog Cymru, the country whose title I have been so greatly privileged to bear during so much of my life and duty. With Catherine beside him, our new Prince and Princess of Wales will, I know, continue to inspire and lead our national conversations, helping to bring the marginal to the centre ground where vital help can be given.

"I want also to express my love for Harry and Meghan as they continue to build their lives overseas.

"In her life of service we saw that abiding love of tradition, together with that fearless embrace of progress, which make us great as nations. The affection, admiration and respect she inspired became the hallmark of her reign. And, as every member of my family can testify, she combined these qualities with warmth, humour and an unerring ability always to see the best in people.

"I pay tribute to my mother's memory and I honour her life of service. I know that her death brings great sadness to so many of you and I share that sense of loss, beyond measure, with you all.

"When the Queen came to the throne, Britain and the world were still coping with the privations and aftermath of the Second World War, and still living by the conventions of earlier times. In the course of the last 70 years we have seen our society become one of many cultures and many faiths. The institutions of the state have changed in turn. But, through all changes and challenges, our nation and the wider family of realms – of whose talents, traditions and achievements I am so inexpressibly proud – have prospered and flourished. Our values have remained, and must remain, constant.

"The role and the duties of Monarchy also remain, as does the sovereign's particular relationship and responsibility towards the Church of England – the church in which my own faith is so deeply rooted.

"In that faith, and the values it inspires, I have been brought up to cherish a sense of duty to others, and to hold in the greatest respect the precious traditions, freedoms and responsibilities of our unique history and our system of parliamentary government.

> *"And to my darling mama, as you begin your last great journey to join my dear late papa, I want simply to say this: thank you. Thank you for your love and devotion to our family and to the family of nations you have served so diligently all these years. May 'flights of angels sing thee to thy rest.'"*

"In a little over a week's time we will come together as a nation, as a Commonwealth and indeed a global community, to lay my beloved mother to rest. In our sorrow, let us remember and draw strength from the light of her example. On behalf of all my family, I can only offer the most sincere and heartfelt thanks for your condolences and support. They mean more to me than I can ever possibly express.

"And to my darling mama, as you begin your last great journey to join my dear late papa, I want simply to say this: thank you. Thank you for your love and devotion to our family and to the family of nations you have served so diligently all these years. May 'flights of angels sing thee to thy rest.'" •

Dedicated
to the
environment

EVEN THOUGH AT TIMES HE WAS RIDICULED, CHARLES HAS ALWAYS
HAD A PASSION FOR SAVING THE PLANET, AND HAS WORKED
TIRELESSLY TO RAISE AWARENESS OF THE ISSUES THE WORLD FACES

W hen it comes to environmental issues, Prince Charles has always been ahead of his time. Indeed, his first speech on the issue was way back in 1968, decades before it was such a hot topic. For having such amazing foresight, he has often been called a visionary.

In 2014 he made a plea for the world to take notice, saying, "The battle against climate change is surely the most defining and pivotal challenge of our time, even in a world full of daunting perils and crises, it is hard to imagine anything that poses a greater challenge and opportunity for humanity. We are running out of time. How many times have I found myself saying this over recent years. We cannot delay, regroup, prevaricate or wait for more or better information. We should compare the planet under threat of climate change to a sick patient. No doctor would wait for 100% certainty while a dying patient slipped away. We cannot ignore the symptoms and should act now to restore the health of the planet before it is too late."

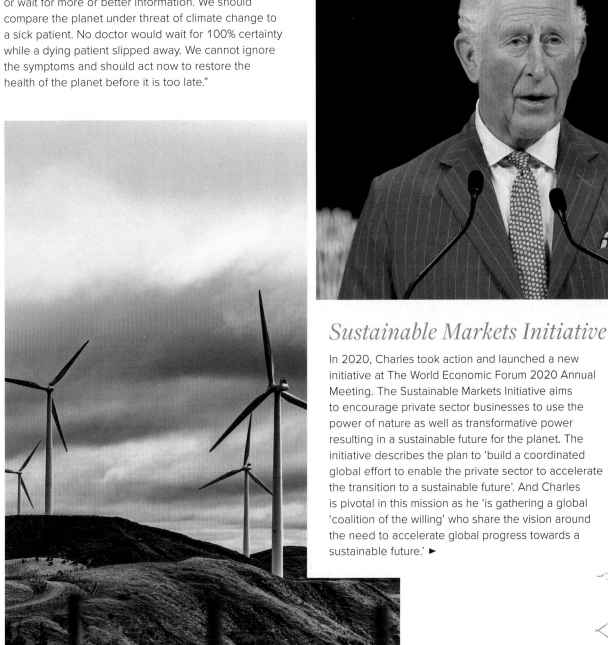

Sustainable Markets Initiative

In 2020, Charles took action and launched a new initiative at The World Economic Forum 2020 Annual Meeting. The Sustainable Markets Initiative aims to encourage private sector businesses to use the power of nature as well as transformative power resulting in a sustainable future for the planet. The initiative describes the plan to 'build a coordinated global effort to enable the private sector to accelerate the transition to a sustainable future'. And Charles is pivotal in this mission as he 'is gathering a global 'coalition of the willing' who share the vision around the need to accelerate global progress towards a sustainable future.' ►

Involvement in COP26

At COP26, the then Prince Charles did not miss the opportunity to reach out to the leaders of the world and implore that they take action. He likened the strategy needed to that of a military one.

The conference was seen as a success, with 40 countries agreeing to stop using coal and almost 200 countries signed the Glasgow Climate Pact which pledges to cut down on the emissions that are leading to global warming.

I can only urge you, as the world's decision-makers, to find practical ways of overcoming differences so we can all get down to work, together, to rescue this precious planet and save the threatened future of our young people.

Highgrove Organic Garden

The Palace describes the beautiful Organic Garden at Highgrove as following Charles' philosophy, 'that it is better to work with Nature than against it.'

On Purchasing Highgrove in the 80s, Charles set about transforming the gardens and setting up a farm, both of which are entirely organic. He then began to sell produce from the farm in the Duchy Originals brand, the proceeds of which went to his charitable causes. ▶

Prince's Rainforests Project

This project was set up by Charles in 2007 in a bid to stop tropical deforestation. In the past, the King has talked about the importance of the world's forests, "Forests... are in fact the world's air-conditioning system, the very lungs of the planet, and help to store the largest body of freshwater on the planet, essential to produce food for our planet's growing population. The rainforests of the world also provide the livelihoods of more than a billion of the poorest people on this Earth. In simple terms, the rainforests, which encircle the world, are our very life-support system-and we are on the verge of switching it off." He said.

Once again, Charles recognises the need for action when it comes to the environment and isn't afraid to say so.

Campaign for Wool

In 2010, Charles became patron of another campaign, this time focussing on wool. The King has always understood that sheep farmers are facing extreme challenges, and so by promoting wool as a sustainable fabric, which biodegrades naturally and won't end up clogging the world's landfills, he manages to incorporate two of his passions into one initiative. •

Like a sleepwalker, we seem unable to wake up to the fact that so many of the catastrophic consequences of carrying on with business-as-usual are bearing down on us faster than we think, already dragging many millions more people into poverty and dangerously weakening global food, water and energy security for the future.

A life of charity

THE KING HAS DEDICATED HIS LIFE
TO IMPROVING THAT OF OTHERS

> *"Every young person deserves a chance to succeed."*

Giving back has been at the core of the King's life ever since he was a boy. During his early years he bore witness to the important charity work his mother and father carried out in communities in both the UK and The Commonwealth.

Charles III has spoken many times about the importance of his charity work, and how it fulfils him more than anything else. "There is nothing more satisfying than seeing the difference you can make to so many young people who have had difficulties and huge disadvantages, and have had unbelievably complicated lives. If you can actually provide them with an opportunity and help them to develop confidence above all, suddenly their lives can be transformed." The King said in the past.

As the Prince of Wales, Charles was patron of hundreds of charities and president of 19 charitable trusts. Much of his charitable focus is on transformation and, vitally, sustaining such transformation. From helping over 1 million disadvantaged young people build confidence and careers to his work in the arts, rural communities, enterprise and of course the environment, charity is a part of who he is.

The Prince's Trust

In the 70s, Charles used his £7,400 severance pay from the Royal Navy to set up The Prince's Trust. The charity aimed to help vulnerable young people, aged 11-30, to prosper in life through a number of training programmes to open up a world of opportunity.

Although head of many charities, it's no secret that The Prince's Trust is particularly close to Charles' heart.

Speaking of his beloved charity, the King has said, "When I created The Prince's Trust in 1976 to help improve the lives of disadvantaged young people, it was because I was so acutely aware of the challenges that they faced. Over the years some of the challenges have changed, but the overall mission of giving people self-confidence and self-esteem and better opportunities remains the same." He continued, "And in that time we've helped over 1 million young people transform their lives. The Prince's Trust now works in 18 countries across The Commonwealth and beyond." ►

The King's eldest son, Prince William, has spoken of his admiration of his father's work with The Prince's Trust. He recently declared, "Some of my earliest memories relate to times when my parents spoke to me, or even better showed me what it meant to have both privilege and responsibility. From my father I learned how essential charity was to his life and his sense of purpose."

The newest Prince of Wales continued, "The Prince's Trust is not an arm's length organisation for my father; he cares deeply about The Prince's Trust because it is a living projection of his values. As a young child I recall evening after evening my feather's diligence and compassion as he applied himself to answering thousands of letters and reading endless reports in order to stay on top of his ambition to do all that he could to help the underprivileged. Without my realising it, what my parents were doing was distilling in me, and Harry, a lifelong habit to put charity at the heart of our lives."

The Prince's Charities

This trust is a combination of the 19 charities Charles is president of, in fact he actually founded 18 of the 19. The name of course comes from his time as The Prince of Wales, before he became King in September 2022.

The charities include:

The Prince's Trust, the work of which is detailed prior. Plus **The Prince's Trust International**, **The Prince's Trust Australia**, **The Prince's Trust Canada**, **The Prince's Trust New Zealand**, **The Prince's Trust America** all of which carry on the good work of the UK branch overseas.
Other charities that focus on opportunities and enterprise include, **The Prince's Scottish Youth Business Trust**, **PRIME**, **PRIME Cymru**, **The Prince's Youth Business International**, **The British Asian Trust** and **Youth Business Scotland**.

He also had many organisations under The Prince's Charities umbrella that focussed on education, the environment and responsible businesses.

"It wasn't easy at the start to set up these charities and organisations to raise money. And like the anonymous poem, 'They said that it could not be done, with a laugh he went right to it. He tackled the thing that couldn't be done, and couldn't do it.' After which I recalled that great Maxim of Ogden Nash, 'If at first you don't succeed, to hell with it.' And so I went on trying."

Now that he is King however, he is likely to take on hundreds more charities as the reigning Monarch. His mother was patron of over 600 charities. In his first speech as King last year, he touched on being less involved with some of his beloved charities, somewhat sadly, saying, "My life will of course change as I take up my new responsibilities. It will no longer be possible for me to give so much of my time and energies to the charities and issues for which I care so deeply. But I know this important work will go on in the trusted hands of others."

And those hands are indeed trusted, as many of the patronages he held as a Prince will likely now be passed to his son and the new heir apparent, Prince William. •

THE QUEEN'S
Coronation

WE DELVE INTO THE ARCHIVES TO EXAMINE THE QUEEN'S
CORONATION AND HOW IT MIGHT DIFFER FROM KING
CHARLES' CELEBRATION

IMAGE CREDIT: SHUTTERSTOCK

On February 7th 1952, while resting after the first week of representing the ailing King George VI on an extensive royal tour, 25-year-old Princess Elizabeth learned that her father had died. The couple were at the Sagana fishing lodge in Kenya when her husband Philip, the Duke of Edinburgh, broke the sad news of his death. Despite her grief, and with great composure and a sense of duty that continued throughout her lifetime, she immediately focussed on the practicalities of her daunting new role.

In a black mourning outfit, the new Queen Elizabeth II returned home to take her Accession Oath at St. James' Palace in London, also saying, "My heart is too full for me to say more to you today than I shall always work, as my father did throughout his reign, to advance the happiness and prosperity of my peoples, spread as they are all the world over."

Aged 11 at her father's Coronation, the new Queen would have known a little of the intricate organisation required for her own, which finally took place on June 2nd 1953. It was the culmination of over a year of detailed planning by a highly skilled team, including the incumbent Earl Marshal, a role which has been undertaken by the Duke of Norfolk for centuries. Bernard Marmaduke Fitzalan-Howard could draw upon the experience of having organised her father's Coronation, yet he still needed 94 diagrams for the purpose of illustrating how each part of the ceremony should run.

Much about the planning upheld centuries of tradition. The location was Westminster Abbey, rebuilt by Henry III specifically as a Coronation church, where all but two Coronations have been held, across nine centuries. The service itself descended directly from King Edgar's in 973, the first English Coronation for which a detailed account still survives, and which has been the blueprint for all subsequent ceremonies. This included the most sacred part of the Coronation, the anointing of the Monarch on the hands, breast and head with holy oil, and the investing of the royal robes and regalia.

The Coronation Weekend - what we know so far

6TH MAY

Whilst many details of the Coronation, known in Royal circles as 'Operation Golden Orb' are a closely-guarded secret, some information has been filtered into the public domain. The Coronation ceremony itself will take place on the 6th of May at Westminster Abbey. During the ceremony both the King and Camilla, the Queen Consort, will be crowned.

It is believed that the Archbishop of Canterbury, Justin Welby, will conduct the ceremony.

The Coronation is a formal ceremony that is both symbolic and religious, but isn't actually a necessary step for a Monarch to be considered King or Queen. In fact, King Edward VIII never actually had a Coronation.

Once the ceremony has taken place, the King and Queen Consort will take part in a royal procession to Buckingham Palace.

Whilst the Coronation is likely to be a spectacular sight, many experts have speculated that the event will be a less grandiose affair than in previous years, due to the current economic condition with many people living in the midst of the cost of living crisis.

7TH MAY

As per other high profile events, the Royal Family are hopeful that the public will join in on the celebrations by holding their own events around Britain. It's hoped that neighbourhoods will gather together in a time of inclusion and friendship to mark the momentous royal occasion. Named 'The Big Coronation Lunch'.

Later that day a splendid concert is scheduled to take place at Windsor Castle and will include performances from the much celebrated Coronation Choir. The choir is made up from a variety of organisations including refugee choirs and LGBTQ choirs. They will perform alongside a second choir which consists of singers from across the commonwealth who will appear by video link. The palace have arranged for thousands of tickets to the concert to be dispensed via ballot to ensure they are distributed fairly. The concert itself will be broadcast by the BBC so the public can enjoy the celebrations from the comfort of their own home.

8TH MAY

To mark the splendid occasion, Britons have been gifted an extra bank holiday. •

Coronation TRADITIONS

ALL EYES WILL BE ON WESTMINSTER ABBEY AS IT HOSTS THE CORONATION OF KING CHARLES III. WORDS BY **CLAIRE SAUL**

On May 6th, the world will witness the Coronation of His Majesty King Charles III at the magnificent Westminster Abbey in London. Since the major rebuilding programme of the Abbey by Henry III in the 13th century, when long transepts were added to allow as many people as possible to witness such events, it has been the designated 'Coronation Church'. To date it has hosted the Coronations of 38 reigning Monarchs spanning almost 1,000 years. Within its walls are many sights and artefacts marking those ceremonies of the past, and awaiting ones ahead.

Key among these is the specific site of the Coronation, one of the Abbey's most treasured possessions. The stunning Cosmati Pavement was laid in 1268 in the mosaic style which had been seen in contemporary Italian churches. Its 80,000 pieces of onyx, porphyry and glass are set into Purbeck marble, arranged in patterns designed to assist the medieval monks in their spiritual contemplation.

If the Cosmati Pavement is one of the Abbey's most precious possessions, The Coronation Chair, usually displayed in St George's Chapel, near the Abbey's West Door, is one of its most famous. It has been the focal point of Coronations for over seven centuries since Edward I ordered its creation in 1297 for the purpose of housing the Stone of Destiny – more familiarly known as the Stone of

Scone – which he had captured in Scotland. The sacred red sandstone stone had been used for centuries for the inauguration of Scottish Monarchs. It remained in England until 1990 before being officially returned to Scotland, where it's displayed in the Crown Room of Edinburgh Castle. It will temporarily return to Westminster Abbey for the King Charles' Coronation.

Originally highly decorated and gilded, the Coronation chair has suffered greatly over time, with elements disappearing, temporary modifications and even bomb damage. There is also historic graffiti carved into it, much of it by the hand of boys from Westminster School and visitors from the 18th and 19th centuries, who used to be allowed to sit in it for a fee.

Treasures on High

A spectacular view can be enjoyed down the length of the Abbey from The Queen's Diamond Jubilee Galleries, located 16 metres above floor level in the triforium on its eastern side. Dating from the 13th century rebuilding work, this space was originally constructed to house a series of chapels, but was never completed. Four hundred years later, Sir Christopher Wren adapted the area for storage and as a space for watching royal events – it is possible to see numbers painted on the walls overlooking the interior of the Abbey, which identify the viewing spots for ticket holders.

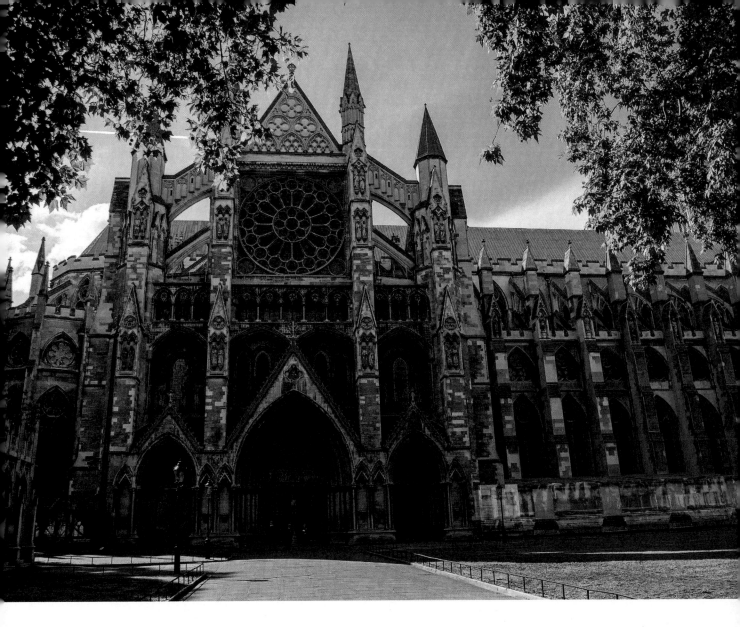

This unique space was reopened in 2018 as a gallery space, where it currently displays 300 items from the Abbey archives, some of them centuries-old items discovered during the construction of the galleries themselves. Amongst these finds were 30,000 pieces of stained glass dating from the medieval building work, some of which now feature in the windows glazing the bridge from the gallery lift, in the purpose-built Weston Tower through which the galleries are accessed.

One of its four display sections looks at the Abbey's close association with the Monarchy and includes some important Coronation-related items. Key among these is the beautifully illustrated 14th century manuscript known as the Liber Regalis (Royal Book), which describes the procedure for staging Coronations and royal funerals. It is thought to have been created in preparation for the crowning of Richard II's consort Anne of Bohemia. Somehow it managed to survive the destruction of the Abbey library during Henry VIII's dissolution of the monasteries, probably due to its importance for those charged with arranging such important ceremonies. The basic format described in the text is the one which has been followed in Coronations ever since.

There is a display of Replica Coronation Regalia, including St Edward's Crown, which is used for the actual crowning of the Sovereign. These were made for use in rehearsals for the 1937 Coronation of the King's grandfather George VI and were also used during the preparations for the late Queen's Coronation in 1953.

By tradition, the new Monarch makes a gift of fabric for the creation of new Coronation Copes for the Abbey's ecclesiastical figures, and examples of such items worn in Coronations spanning the last three centuries are also displayed here. On Elizabeth II's Coronation, the incumbent Dean decided against wearing the new blue cope made for him and plumped instead for the crimson velvet cope decorated with stars and flowers which had been created for Charles II's 1661 Coronation. The crowning of William III and Mary II in 1689 as joint rulers demanded the creation of a second Coronation chair. The Coronation Chair of Mary II was designed with the original, Edward I model in mind. Even though the queen had a stronger claim to the throne than her husband, it was she who used this second chair during their Coronation. Like its even older counterpart, it is covered in historic graffiti.

The large oil painting The Coronation Theatre: Portrait of HM Queen Elizabeth II has even greater emotional resonance, since her passing. Australian artist Ralph Heimans' stunning work depicts the late queen in an imagined scene in later life, contemplating the spot on the Cosmati pavement where she was crowned. It was ►

purchased for the Abbey to mark her Diamond Jubilee.

Before leaving the galleries, visitors should take a few moments to enjoy the spectacular views through the high Abbey windows and across the carvings of the exterior masonry, to Parliament Square and the Houses of Parliament.

Operation Golden Orb

The King has declared his intent to have a slimmed down version of the Coronation, an event which will be the product of meticulous plans. These are a closely guarded secret and have allegedly been drawn up under the code name Operation Golden Orb. Although Coronations are held in Westminster Abbey, they are State occasions and therefore not organised by the Dean and Chapter of the Abbey but under the authority of the Earl Marshal, a role which has traditionally been undertaken by the Duke of Norfolk for centuries. It is a highly detailed and complicated project. Bernard Fitzalan-Howard already had the experience of organising George VIs Coronation when he was tasked with the late Queen's, yet he still required no less than 94 diagrams to illustrate how each part of the ceremony should run.

The Archbishop of Canterbury, the Most Reverend Justin Welby, is the person tasked with preparing the order of service, officiating during the ceremony and conducting the actual crowning of King Charles and his Queen Consort. He will be assisted by the Dean of Westminster, Dr David Hoyle, who also performs the role of instructing the Sovereign about matters relating to the ceremony.

Coronation Haps & Mishaps

All Coronations are memorable occasions. Some have been remarkable for unique circumstances and others for occurrences that even their generous budgets and intricate planning have not been able to circumvent.

William the Conqueror's ceremony in 1066 is the first recorded Coronation at Westminster Abbey, the location chosen to underline his claim as the rightful successor of Edward the Confessor, who is buried there. It took place on December 25th, William choosing to associate himself with this special spiritual day. It was a tense and hurried event, the only celebratory noise around the Abbey coming from the Norman's own men. During the ceremony the loud shouts of the congregation as they gave their assent to the new king, alarmed William's French-speaking guards outside. They assumed the start of a riot, possibly an assassination. They set fire to surrounding houses and as smoke began to infiltrate the Abbey, the congregation fled in panic. The Coronation needed to be completed in great haste, the new king 'trembling from head to foot'.

The 1220 Coronation of Henry III at Westminster Abbey was actually his second – he had first been crowned at Gloucester Abbey, at the tender age of nine. The occasion set the precedent that the succession of the Monarchy passed automatically to the outgoing Monarch's eldest son, regardless of their age. The presence of Royal favourite Piers Gaveston at the Coronation of Edward II in 1308 caused a great deal of discontent and not only due to the nature of their relationship. During the ceremony Gaveston flouted protocol, walking in front of the king in the procession and carrying the crown of St Edward the Confessor in his own hands.

Henry IV (1399) initiated the Coronation tradition of creating Knights of the Bath, named after the symbolically purifying baths taken before the men received their honour. Henry also initiated the Coronation procedure of anointment with sacred oil and was the first to be enthroned on the 'Stone of Scone'.

Henry VIII wore a typically splendid set of crimson robes to his 1509 Coronation and walked there along a flower and herb-strewn striped cloth, which was shredded for souvenirs by the crowds as soon as he entered the Abbey. His daughter Mary I (1553) refused to sit in the same Coronation chair as her 'heretic' Protestant half-brother and predecessor Edward VI and had a new one made for her. She also sent for holy oil from Europe, to ensure that she was not anointed with the same oil as had been used in his ceremony. Her half-sister Elizabeth I consulted her astrologer to set the date for her Coronation in 1559, while a devastating outbreak of plague delayed her successor James I's in 1603 and numbers were limited due to the fear of infection. Charles II's Coronation was notable for many reasons, one being the first appearance of much of the Coronation regalia we still see today, commissioned by the king for his ceremony in 1661 after the restoration of the Monarchy.

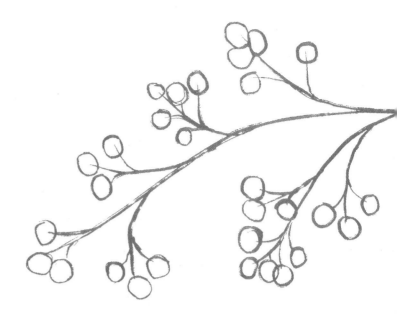

When James II's crown slipped off his head in 1685 and the Royal Standard at the Tower of London was torn by the wind, it was viewed by many as a portent of things to come. Hanoverian George I (1714) had little English and the attending officials could not speak German, so they tried to struggle by in Latin. When he tried to repeat a declaration required by the ceremony, the strength of his accent meant that witnesses to the event could not understand him. George II (1727) found himself very uncomfortable in his resplendent Coronation regalia on an unseasonably warm October day. His ermine-lined crimson velvet cap was not only hot but too large and repeatedly fell over his eyes. The choir also managed to burst into Handel's Zadok the Priest, the Coronation anthem, at the wrong moment in the ceremony. George III's Coronation (1761) was a lengthy affair and a very disorganised one. When the Archbishop of Canterbury started to deliver his sermon, the congregation took the opportunity to consume the food and wine they had brought along, to the accompaniment of clattering plates and cutlery. George IV (1821) also overheated on his extravagant Coronation day, and needed multiple handkerchiefs to mop his brow. Probably adding to his perspiration was the commotion caused by his estranged wife Queen Caroline. George had refused to allow her to attend and she suffered the humiliation of being locked out of the Abbey, the guards refusing her entry at every door she tried.

In complete contrast to the decadence of this immediate predecessors, William IV was reluctant to have a Coronation at all and only agreed on the condition that as little money was spent on it as possible, leading some to refer to the 1831 event as the 'Half-Crownation', despite the fact that the equivalent of £2 million today was spent on it.

During the 1838 Coronation of Queen Victoria, the Archbishop tried to force her bespoke Coronation ring onto the wrong finger, causing her to wince in pain. An elderly peer tumbled down the steps while paying homage to the new Monarch and an attending bishop concluded the ceremony prematurely by mistake. Victoria was required to go back and complete the missing section before processing out of the Abbey.

Appendicitis and peritonitis required an operation which delayed the crowning of Edward VII in 1902 and abdication meant that the Coronation of Edward VIII did not happen at all. Stepping into his shoes on the designated 1937 date was his younger brother George VI. Guests began arriving at 6am for the lavish ceremony that day, some even tucking sandwiches under their coronets to sustain them through the many hours ahead. Amongst several unplanned incidents during the event, The Archbishop of Canterbury almost placed St Edward's Crown the wrong way round on the king's head, one bishop accidentally stepped on his train and another managed to cover the words of the oath with his thumb, just as the King prepared to read it.

Reflections on '53

The King can recall the Coronation of his late mother, 70 years ago. He once stated, "I have vivid memories of the Coronation. I remember my mother coming to say goodnight to my sister and me while wearing the crown so that she could get used to its weight on her head before the Coronation ceremony. I recall thousands of people gathered in The Mall outside Buckingham Palace chanting 'We want the Queen' and keeping me awake at night." The [then] four-year-old prince received his own, personalised invitation to the event, hand-painted with soldiers playing musical instruments. He witnessed the ceremony tucked in-between his grandmother the Queen Mother, and his aunt, Princess Margaret.

May 6th, 2023

Hopefully no such incidents will befall King Charles' Coronation this May. According to statements from Buckingham Palace, we can expect a ceremony that reflects the monarch's role as it stands today and which also looks ahead towards the future, while including the key traditions and pageantry that have run through those of his predecessors across the centuries.

Along with his early memories of witnessing his young mother practising with the weighty crowns before her ceremony, the King can also recall her "amazing poise" and "natural grace", qualities which, amongst many others, he will be hoping to emulate on this great historic day. •

FOR MORE DETAILS ON WESTMINSTER ABBEY VISIT WESTMINSTER-ABBEY.ORG, WHICH INCLUDES FURTHER INFORMATION ABOUT THE QUEEN'S DIAMOND JUBILEE GALLERIES.

CORONATION
JEWELS AND REGALIA

CLAIRE SAUL LOOKS AT THE SHINIEST, SPARKLIEST STARS OF THE CORONATION CEREMONY.

A coronation cannot proceed without royal regalia, the ultimate symbols of the Monarch's status. Playing a central role at events on May 6th, as they have done for every Coronation since that of Charles II in 1661, will be the star items from the magnificent Crown Jewels.

The use of state regalia originates many centuries earlier than 1661, but the events of the English Civil War had a devastating effect on the items employed. Shortly after King Charles I was executed in 1649, these symbolic and valuable so-called 'Toys and Trifles' of Monarchy were defaced and stripped of their precious jewels and delivered to the Royal Mint inside the Tower of London, to be melted down into coin. Other items were sold off, along with the King's vast collection of art, which was dispersed throughout Europe.

But political turmoil followed Oliver Cromwell's death and in 1660 Parliament invited the exiled Charles II back, to be crowned King. Plans were swiftly made for a lavish Coronation that befitted the restoration of the Monarchy.

Charles was fully aware of the importance of tradition and magnificence in enforcing his right to the throne and his authority as a ruler and Head of the Church. He directed discussions about the creation of new royal regalia and spent £13,000 – the equivalent cost of three fully-equipped warships – on eleven key items for his 1661 Coronation. Many of these pieces are still in use today, although they have had modifications over the years.

The Crown Jewels now comprise over 100 sacred and ceremonial objects, featuring over 23,000 gemstones. As part of the Royal Collection, they are held in trust by the Monarch for the nation and retained on secure display at the Tower of London's Jewel House.

Jewels at the Coronation

On the eve of the Coronation, the items of the Coronation Regalia are transported from the Tower of London to Westminster Abbey, where they are guarded overnight. The following morning, the Abbey clergy take them through the cloisters and into the church in procession. Most of the regalia is placed on the High Altar, but the Imperial State Crown is taken to the altar in St Edward's Chapel, at the heart of the Abbey.

During the most sacred part of the ceremony, the Sovereign is anointed with holy oil, poured from the eagle-shaped Ampulla into the Coronation Spoon, into which the Archbishop of Canterbury dips his fingers to anoint the Sovereign. This 12th century spoon is the only surviving item from the medieval set of Coronation Regalia, having escaped the melting pot at the Royal Mint after being sold for 16 shillings to an official of Charles I's Wardrobe. He very sensibly returned it to Charles II for use in his 1661 Coronation.

The Sovereign is invested with regalia symbolising the chivalric nature of kingship. The Spurs are fashioned in the style of medieval spurs, and while in past centuries they were attached to the feet of the Sovereign, they are now only symbolically held to the feet. The Sword of Offering is a later piece, based on George IV's own design and first used at his 1821 Coronation. The sword's jewel-encrusted

scabbard alone includes 2,000 diamonds, alongside rubies, emeralds and sapphires which are set into a repeating pattern of roses, thistles and shamrocks. The original 1661 enamelled Armills are two 'bracelets of sincerity and wisdom', thought to relate to ancient symbols of knighthood and military leadership. They are decorated with the emblems of England, Scotland, Ireland and Wales. King Charles III may well use the brand-new pair that his mother Elizabeth II wore for her 1953 coronation, which were created as a gift from the Commonwealth.

The golden Sovereign's Orb features bands of diamonds, emeralds, pearls, rubies and sapphires which divide it onto three sections representing the three continents known in the medieval age. The item represents the Sovereign's power and its cross, mounted on the top of the globe, symbolises the Christian world. The Sovereign's Ring will be placed on The King's fourth finger of his right hand, according to tradition. This sapphire ring with its ruby cross was created for William IV's Coronation in 1831. It has been worn at every Coronation since, with the exception of Queen Victoria's, whose small fingers required the creation of a bespoke piece.

Also dating from Charles II's 1661 regalia are the Sovereign's Sceptre with Cross, which represents temporal power and is associated with good governance, and the Sceptre with the Dove, symbolising spiritual authority. The former has been adapted over the centuries, most notably in 1911 to incorporate the 530-carat Cullinan I diamond, the largest colourless cut diamond in the world.

The undoubted star of the show is St Edward's Crown,

Theft at the Tower

Self-appointed 'Colonel' Thomas Blood was a complicated character. The smooth-talking former soldier was a reckless and violent adventurer while at the same time, a deeply religious man. He had lived a prosperous life in Ireland after the Civil War but after some of his lands were confiscated, he led a vendetta against the Lord Lieutenant of Ireland, the Duke of Ormonde, whom he held personally responsible.

But Blood is best known in the history books for his audacious attempt to steal the Crown Jewels. He was a familiar face at the Tower of London, having already made several visits, disguised as a clergyman, to befriend the elderly Jewel House Keeper, Talbot Edwards. So there was no reason to doubt his presence when he, his 'wealthy nephew' and their accomplices arrived at the Tower of London in May 1671, under the guise of introducing the 'nephew' to Talbot's unmarried daughter.

As they waited in Edwards' rooms, Blood asked to see the Crown Jewels, something that was not uncommon at a time when for a fee, visitors could even handle these precious items. Edwards obliged but the poor man was attacked, Blood and his cronies using weapons they had smuggled in. They seized the Imperial State Crown and the Orb, which was unceremoniously stuffed down the breeches of one of the accomplices, and also the Sovereign's Sceptre with Cross, which they started to try and file in half, to be smuggled out in the same way.

Fate intervened in the form of Edwards' son who arrived home unexpectedly from Flanders at that very point, discovering Blood and his men. The alarm was raised as the thugs tried to dash from the Tower to reach their horses. They were eventually captured, but not before a scuffle and an exchange of fire with the Tower guards.

Astonishingly, Blood escaped punishment. After being granted an audience with King Charles II, he was not only released and pardoned for all his crimes but was awarded a grant of Irish lands worth £500 each year - that smooth-talking was evidently put to good use, once more. Already a government informer, he continued his work as a spy. Poor Talbot Edwards was offered £300 for his injuries. The recompense was never fully paid. ►

named after its medieval predecessor, destroyed in 1649, that dated back to 11th century king, Edward the Confessor. St Edward's Crown is placed on the Sovereign's head at the precise moment of Coronation.

The jewel-encrusted, solid gold crown weighs in at a hefty 2.23kg and replicates the original's four crosses-pattée, four fleurs-de-lis and two arches. It also features a purple velvet cap and a band of ermine. It was set with hired stones for coronations until that of George V in 1911, when it was permanently set with semi-precious stones.

At the conclusion of the Coronation, the Monarch withdraws to St Edward's Chapel to be cloaked in a robe of purple velvet. St Edward's Crown is replaced with the lighter Imperial State Crown, still a weighty 1.06kg. Created in 1937 for the Coronation of King George VI, it includes 2,868 diamonds, 269 pearls, 17 sapphires and 11 emeralds. Many of these stones have their own fascinating history, including the late Queen's declared favourite, the large red spinel known as the 'Black Prince's Ruby' which, it has been claimed, was awarded to Edward III's son in the 14th century and subsequently worn by Henry V at the Battle of Agincourt. Possibly, like the Coronation Spoon, it was also sold in 1649 and returned after the Restoration. So too perhaps was the oldest gem in the royal collection, St. Edward's sapphire which, according to legend, was originally worn in a ring of Edward the Confessor. The 104-carat blue Stuart Sapphire is thought to have been smuggled out of the country by King James II when he fled England

in 1688. It took 130 years to return to royal possession. The 317-carat Cullinan II is the second largest of the nine large stones and 97 brilliants of the Cullinan Diamond given to Edward VII on his 66th birthday by the government of the Transvaal - a former British crown colony - in present day South Africa.

No doubt King Charles III will practise with the crowns, just as his late mother did before him in 1953. Former lady-in-waiting Lady Anne Glenconner attended that ceremony as a maid of honour. In a 2021 interview she recalled that after the ceremony, the [then] four-year-old Prince Charles picked up the priceless Imperial State Crown from a table at Buckingham Palace. Luckily it was retrieved from his little fingers before any damage could be done.

Presumably our new Queen Consort will also rehearse with the crown she will receive during the Coronation ceremony.

Possibly it will be the platinum and diamond Crown of Queen Elizabeth the Queen Mother, which features the Koh-i-nûr ('Mountain of Light'), presented to Queen Victoria in 1850 from the Treasury of Lahore, and one of the most famous – and controversial – diamonds in the world. Perhaps she will also wear the Queen Consort's Coronation Ring, originally made for William IV's consort Queen Adelaide almost two hundred years ago. The deep pink ruby and diamond piece was also worn by Charles' grandmother at King George VI's Coronation in 1937.

The Gold State Coach

Tucked into the grounds of Buckingham Palace is the Royal Mews, the department of the Royal Household responsible for two high profile means of travel for the Royal Family – the fleet of royal limousines and the horse drawn coaches and carriages that are admired on grand state and family occasions.

The Royal Mews is open to visitors, who can view of some of the elegant carriages held in the Royal Collection and discover more about them. Queen Alexandra's State Coach, for example, is recognisable as the means of conveying the Imperial State Crown and other regalia to the annual State Opening of Parliament. The magnificent Diamond Jubilee State Coach incorporates materials sourced from over one hundred historic sites and organisations, including the late Queen's beloved Royal Yacht Britannia, elements from Isaac Newton's apple tree and Henry VIIIs flagship The Mary Rose. Nestling below the pale gold silk brocade seats is even a piece of the Stone of Scone.

Undoubtedly the star attraction and the biggest talking point at the Royal Mews is the Gold State Coach, commissioned for George III in 1760, for the occasion of his coronation and his wedding to Princess Charlotte of Mecklenburg-Strelitz, but unfortunately not completed until two years later. Used for every coronation since that of his son George IV in 1821, this 261-year-old gilded statement of opulence weighs four tonnes, is 7.3m long and requires eight strong horses, always Windsor Greys, to draw it. They wear the special Red Morocco State Harness, which is reserved especially for use with this coach.

There is a lot to digest, not least the enormous carved Tritons at each of its wheels. which represent imperial power. On the roof, three cherubs represent the guardian spirits of England, Scotland and Ireland. They support a golden Royal Crown and brandish the Sceptre, the Sword of State and the Ensign of Knighthood. The decorative side panels of the coach were created by the Florentine artist Giovanni Battista Cipriani and feature Roman gods and goddesses, the central three of which are holding the Imperial Crown of Great Britain. The panels provide a contrast to the gilded sprouting palm trees, lions heads and symbols of British victory in war which make up the body of the coach.

The coach is made of giltwood – a layer of gold leaf over wood – and has been modified and improved over time. For the late Queen's Coronation it had supports fitted to carry the heavy orb and sceptre, positioned to give the impression that she was carrying them. It is believed that staff from the Royal Mews fixed a hot water bottle under the seat for comfort, as it was such an unseasonably cold and wet day. We most recently saw it at the Platinum Jubilee Pageant, when it was temporarily updated with a hologram of the Queen on her Coronation day, waving through the windows.

As you watch the Gold State Coach travel to the Coronation, consider the skills and forbearance of several people. There is precious little turning room in the dedicated Gold State Coach House at the Royal Mews and more pertinently, none of the doors in that house are wide enough to accommodate the 3.9m height and 2.5m width of the coach. Those charged with handling it are required to remove an entire section of the long wall of the Coach House, an operation that takes 30 people two days to complete. The coach also has a stopping distance of 27m, even after the brake handle is applied, requiring a skilled degree of manipulation for those driving it under the gaze of the world, on Coronation Day.

And spare a thought for our new monarch and his Queen Consort, too. Despite improvements over the years, it's a famously uncomfortable ride. William IV compared it to being aboard a ship "tossing in a rough sea". Queen Victoria complained of "distressing oscillation" while the late Queen Elizabeth referred to her experience of riding in it, as "horrible… not very comfortable." •

THE ROYAL MEWS IS OPEN MARCH 2 - OCTOBER 30 THIS YEAR BUT CLOSED TO THE PUBLIC ON CERTAIN DAYS FOR ROYAL DUTIES. CHECK ALL DETAILS AT RCT.UK/VISIT/ROYALMEWS

60 facts about
KING CHARLES

FROM THE EXACT TEMPERATURE HE PREFERS HIS TEA, TO HOW MANY MILITARY
REGIMENTS HIS MAJESTY IS AFFILIATED WITH, AND EVERYTHING IN BETWEEN,
WE DIVULGE THE LESSER KNOWN FACTS ABOUT THE NEW KING

Charles became the heir apparent aged just three, and is the longest serving Prince of Wales in history.

King Charles was actually the 23rd Prince of Wales before Prince William took over.

His first official trip abroad was when he was age five and visited Malta.

As well as attending Cambridge University, the King also attended University College of Wales, where he learned how to speak the Welsh language.

Charles has, on occasion, puts his time at the University College of Wales to use by speaking in Welsh during official speeches.

Charles plays the cello very well, even performing in a symphony concert at Cambridge whilst he studied there.

The King became the first ever heir apparent to earn a university degree, first obtaining a Bachelor's Degree and then later a Master's Degree.

Charles enjoyed acting as a boy, he played the lead in *Macbeth* whilst at secondary school.

His Majesty also joined a drama group, the Dryden Society, whilst at Trinity College Cambridge, where he performed on stage regularly.

He has a certificate of merit in ice skating, having learned in 1962 at Richmond Ice Rink.

Food & drink

Charles won't allow Foie Gras to be served in his household. As the making of the dish involves geese being force-fed, he finds it to be unnecessarily cruel.

Charles is said to be exacting about how his tea is served. His former Hospitality manager revealed that the water for green tea must be 70 degrees exactly (a thermometer is used to be sure) and 100 degrees for Earl Grey.

He also has preferences for how long the tea should be brewed — green tea for three minutes and black tea for five.

The King prefers not to eat lunch.

One of his favourite dishes is 'groussaka', which is the same as the Greek dish moussaka, but made with grouse instead of the traditional lamb.

He also loves the humble boiled egg and is said to eat one every single day.

His preferred breakfast is mixed wheat germ and cereal grains with honey.

Charles set up his own food company in 1990 named Duchy Organics. The brand can still be found at Waitrose.

In fact, he was passionate about organic food and the health benefits, some 30 years before it became as trendy as it is now.

Charles and Camilla often take their own alcohol with them whilst touring both in the UK and abroad. Charles enjoys a gin and tonic whilst Camilla prefers a good red wine. ▶

Residences

Clarence House has previously been the official London residence of Charles.

Birkhall in Scotland is where Charles and Camilla often spend their summer breaks.

Before his marriage to Diana, Charles bought Highgrove House in Gloucestershire. Now Charles and Camilla enjoy staying there often. The gardens have been open to the public since 1996.

Highgrove House has somewhat of a tragic history. Back in the 1800s, the granddaughter of the then owner sadly died after her gown caught on fire during a grand ball.

The King may soon move to Buckingham Palace, following in the footsteps of his late mother.

Little-known facts

When dignitaries visit the US, they are given a codename by the Secret Service. Charles is said to have been bestowed the name 'Unicorn'.

In the early 70s, it's reported that then President Nixon, made a not particularly subtle attempt to set up his daughter with the heir apparent. Tricia was seated next to Charles at nearly every event the Prince attended, but the plan did not work as the pair didn't hit it off.

Charles is said not to have a mobile phone, one of the few people in the world who do not.

The king struck up a surprising friendship with Barbara Streisand. Having been a big fan, he met with the singer and actress on the set of Funny Lady and they got on famously. Streisand has since said, "We became friends, and I loved spending some time at Highgrove for a weekend fundraiser and going through his gardens."

Charles has a species of frog named after him. In 2012 a new species of Ecuadorian Tree Frog was found and given the name the Prince Charles stream tree frog, to honour his work in rainforest conservation.

Charles has revealed that his car runs on 'wine and cheese'. The car uses a high blend of bioethanol made from cheese and wine. Charles said, "My old Aston Martin, which I've had for 51 years, runs on – can you believe this – surplus English white wine, and whey from the cheese process."

He is widely known as being somewhat of a workaholic. In fact, his son, Prince Harry, once commented, "This is a man who has dinner ridiculously late at night, and then goes to his desk later that night and will fall asleep on his notes to the point where he'll wake up with a piece of paper stuck to his face." Camilla has since commented that Charles works so hard because, "he would like to change the world."

Charles is a published children's author. In the 80s he wrote 'The Old Man of Lochnagar', about a Scottish man who meets a God of the sea.

He is said to be a skilled magician. In fact, in 1975 he performed a difficult trick to earn a coveted membership to the Magic Circle, an association of magicians.

He is an advocate of talking to plants. Charles said, "I happily talk to plants and trees and listen to them. I think it's absolutely crucial." He also shakes the branches of new trees he plants for good luck. ▶

Military

His Majesty is affiliated with 18 military regiments.

Whilst studying in his second year at Cambridge, Charles requested Royal Air Force training. By 1971 he was able to fly himself to the Royal Air Force College where he trained as a jet pilot.

Charles was the first member of The Royal Family to obtain his RAF wings as Flight Lieutenant Wales in August 1971.

He is a trained jet and helicopter pilot.

His first Service appointment was in 1969 as Colonel-in-Chief of the Royal Regiment of Wales.

He completed a course at Royal Naval College, Dartmouth.

Charles became Admiral of the Fleet of The Royal Navy.

His Majesty served on HMS Norfolk, the frigates HMS Minerva and HMS Jupiter.

He later commanded HMS Bronington in 1976.

He completed the Parachute Regiment's training course, the first member of the Royal Family to do so. He was later appointed Colonel-in-Chief of the Regiment in 1977.

Charity

Charles is President or Patron of over 420 charities including ActionAid, The Prince's Trust and The British Forces Foundation.

The Prince's Trust has helped over 875,000 disadvantaged young people find employment.

He actually set up The Prince's Trust in 1976 using his severance pay from the Navy, which amounted to £7,400.

The King's charity work has come a long way. His charities now raise over £140 million for various causes each year.

Waitrose Duchy Organics (which Charles originally set up), donates £3million annually to The Prince's Trust.

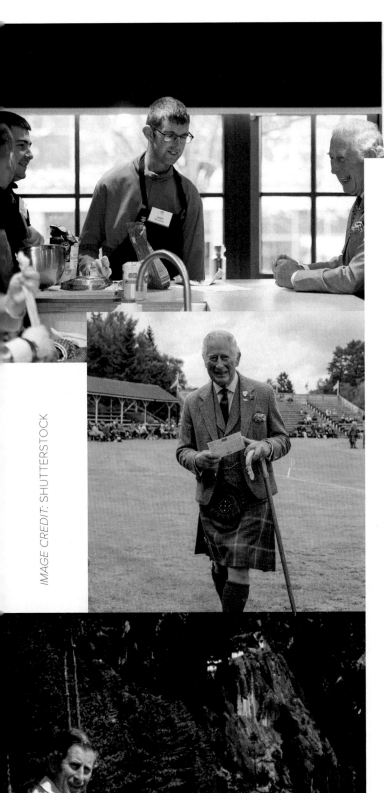

Charles' first ever Royal engagement was back in 1965 at the Palace of Holyroodhouse.

He has visited almost 100 countries around the world.

The King is a keen artist. He anonymously submitted a watercolour to Royal Academy of Arts, which was then displayed in their 1987 Summer Exhibition.

Charles and Camilla appeared in The Beano comic in 2013.

Charles has presented the Weather on BBC.

He's also made a cameo on Coronation Street.

Charles has written books on the environment including one called, 'Harmony: A New Way of Looking at Our World.'

In 2009, Charles was named The Best Dressed Man in the UK in 2009 by Esquire magazine.

He has 32 Godchildren and counting.

Charles and his son William now never fly on the same plane in case they were both to perish in a crash. •

Camilla,
QUEEN CONSORT

CAMILLA HAS WEATHERED MANY A STORM IN THE
CHANGING TIDE OF PUBLIC OPINION. **WORDS BY CLAIRE SAUL**

> *"I count on the loving help of my darling wife, Camilla. In recognition of her own loyal public service since our marriage 17 years ago, she becomes my Queen Consort. I know she will bring to the demands of her new role the steadfast devotion to duty on which I have come to rely so much."*

King Charles III, September 2022

When a mutual friend introduced Camilla Shand and the Prince of Wales in 1970, she jokingly cautioned them about their 'genetic antecedents'; Camilla's great-grandmother Alice Keppel was the mistress of the Prince's great-great-grandfather, King Edward VII. Their descendants had immediate rapport, their ensuing friendship blossoming into an 18-month love affair.

Charles later admitted that he had realised that Camilla was his soulmate in life, but it was not to be. The relationship concluded for undisclosed reasons but significantly, neither the Prince's valued confidante Lord Mountbatten, nor his parents Queen Elizabeth II and the Duke of Edinburgh sanctioned it, while his grandmother Queen Elizabeth the Queen Mother was eager for Charles to marry into the Spencer family. During 1973, Charles was sent away on Royal Navy duty and Camilla married Andrew Parker Bowles, a society wedding attended by the senior members of the Royal Family.

The next chapters of their lives are a familiar story that has been picked over and dramatised hundreds of times and with varying degrees of accuracy and bias. Fast forward to 1995 when the Parker Bowles's divorced, as did the Wales the following year, the couple having resumed their relationship. Camilla was cast as a marriage wrecker and public opinion was poor. Disapproval came from the Palace too, although there were some unlikely and influential allies, including the [then] Archbishop of Canterbury and the editor of one sensationalist tabloid newspaper who admitted after meeting Camilla, "She's bright, switched on and tuned in to the modern world... She is exactly what the Monarchy needs."

Camilla was anxious and deeply hurt by many years of vile, personal attacks and the public dissection of her personal life, yet bore it with quiet dignity, navigating events thoughtfully and carefully. Her relationship with the two young Princes, especially after the tragic death of their mother in 1997 was a particular concern, but new hope sprang with the prominent position they gave her at the 50th birthday party they arranged for their father following year. In 1999, the couple appeared in public for the first time together, the first of many carefully choreographed public appearances as a couple.

The Church of England's 2002 decision to accept second marriages for divorced spouses marked a significant turning point for Charles and Camilla. Subsequently, the Archbishop of Canterbury, declared that he would "happily preside over their union." Finally with his parents' announcement of their "warmest good wishes" for the couple, they became engaged in 2005, Camilla receiving a platinum and diamond engagement ring passed down from the Queen. Henceforth she would be titled Her Royal Highness, The Duchess of Cornwall.

Dispelling the bride's understandable anxiety about public reaction, around 20,000 cheering people lined the streets of Windsor when in April 2005, the couple's 35-year relationship culminated in a civil marriage ceremony at the Guildhall. The Queen was among the guests joining them at the following Service of Prayer and Dedication at St George's Chapel, at Windsor Castle. She also hosted their reception in the state apartments there, and in a speech full of horse racing analogy, remarked on their endurance of all that had challenged them, adding, "...they have come through and I'm very proud and wish them well. My son is home and dry with the woman he loves." The groom was ▶

full of emotion, telling the assembled guests of his bride, "She has stood with me through thick and thin and [her] optimism and humour have seen me through."

Recognition of her subsequent years of diligence and dedicated work by Charles' side at home and abroad, came in April 2012, when the Queen appointed the Duchess as a Dame Grand Cross of the Royal Victorian Order, a prestigious honour recognising distinguished personal service to the Monarch. The Queen's strides in accepting and valuing her daughter-in-law over the years were in no small part influential in improving the minds of the public, too. Camilla was recognised as the rock that Charles needed in his life, accompanying him on work engagements, sharing confidences and supporting him through the pressures of his notoriously busy work schedule.

In February 2022, the Queen said, "I was blessed that in Prince Philip I had a partner willing to carry out the role of consort and unselfishly make the sacrifices that go with it. It is a role I saw my own mother perform during my father's reign... And when, in the fullness of time, my son Charles becomes King, I know you will give him and his wife Camilla the same support that you have given me; and it is my sincere wish that, when the time comes, Camilla will be known as Queen Consort as she continues her own loyal service."

Camilla's path to Queen Consort has been one of extraordinary twists and turns, conducted under the intense scrutiny of the world's media. It has seen royal disapproval turn to acceptance and endorsement and public vilification finally turn to approval, all set against the backdrop of Charles' enduring love for her. Through this she has steadily embraced a role requiring a total change in lifestyle and responsibility, all the while, gently feeling her way as a stepmother to the two Princes and step-grandmother to their families, while remaining a devoted mother and grandmother to her own. She is often seen as a role model for mature women; comfortable in her own skin, and able to deploy the wisdom and skills garnered through her years of life experience.

And so it is that Camilla will be crowned Queen Consort at the side of King Charles III in May. Like her husband, she takes on this enormous responsibility in her mid-70s.

"The Duke of Edinburgh's philosophy was clear: 'Look up and look out, say less, do more – and get on with the job'," Camilla explained last year. "And that is just what I intend to do."

Sweet Charity

Since 2007, The Queen Consort has hosted an annual Christmas party for terminally ill children and their families, where traditional activities include the dressing of a large Christmas tree. It is obviously an occasion close to her heart, Camilla once referring to it as, "one of the most special things we do all year."

Camilla gives her support to around 100 charities as their Patron or President, many of them associated with certain prevailing themes, including health and well-being and the support of survivors of rape, sexual assault and domestic violence. Animal welfare is another key category. Through her role as Patron of Battersea Dogs and Cats Home, one of several patronages passed on to Camilla from the Queen, the household head count has grown by two, in the form of Beth and Bluebell, much loved dogs. Other high-profile patronages awarded to her at that time included Barnardo's and The Royal School of Needlework.

Camilla is passionate about literacy, recognising its personal worth and its ability to change and improve people's lives. Examples of these patronages include the National Literacy Trust and children's reading charity BookTrust.

Of great personal significance to Camilla, as the daughter, wife and stepmother of former military personnel are her military patronages, including the War Memorials Trust and The Poppy Factory, which assists disabled veterans into work with many businesses throughout the UK. When Prince Philip transferred his role as colonel-in-chief of The Rifles to Camilla, she described it as, "one of the greatest honours of my life."

Family also bonds her to the Royal Osteoporosis Society, a charity she has supported for many years, having lost both her grandmother and her mother through the disorder. Since 2001 she has served as the charity's President.

Most Recent Queen Consorts

Alexandra of Denmark's 1863 marriage to Edward Albert, Prince of Wales propelled her into the full glare of public life, his mother Queen Victoria having retreated into an extended period of mourning after her husband's death. A devoted wife to the man who became King Edward VII, Alexandra was involved with many philanthropic works and became president of the Queen Alexandra's Royal Nursing Corps, named after her, which still thrives today.

Known to her family as 'May', Victoria Mary of Teck was a great granddaughter of George III. She was originally engaged to Edward and Alexandra's eldest son Albert Victor, but after his sudden death, eventually wed his younger brother George in 1893. The couple shared a happy and devoted marriage, becoming King George V and Queen Mary in 1910. An enduring and staunch support as his Queen Consort - he claimed that he would be lost without her guidance and commitment - Mary was particularly recognised for her support of servicemen during the First World War.

Elizabeth Bowes-Lyon married Prince Albert, Duke of York in 1923, who described her as "the most marvellous person in the world in my eyes". After King George V's death in 1936, fate intervened with the abdication of Albert's elder brother, casting the reluctant couple into their new role as King George VI and Queen Consort. They were devoted in their responsibilities to the nation and to each other. Elizabeth continued to perform public duties after the king's death, and was a much loved and influential figure in Prince Charles' life. •

BY ROYAL
Appointment

CLAIRE SAUL LOOKS AT THE PRESTIGIOUS
HONOURS KNOWN AS ROYAL WARRANTS, THE
ULTIMATE SEAL OF APPROVAL FOR BUSINESSES

Every business thrives on positive endorsement and when it arrives in the form of a Royal Warrant, it marks product or service quality and recognition of which every owner and employee can be proud. Permission to display the Royal Arms on a company wall or above a door, on stationery, products, packaging, marketing material and websites, delivers an invaluable sense of company pride and commitment.

Generally, around 850 warrant holders have the honour of this royal recognition, covering an extensive cross section of trade and industry, and supplying a variety of items and services ranging from luxury items to the same practical, household items to be found in any home, be it castle or cottage. The vast majority of them belong to the Royal Warrant Holders Association (RWHA), an organisation which for almost two hundred years has sought to 'ensure the continued existence of Royal Warrants as a treasured and respected institution'. It also administers new applications for warrants, amendments to existing ones and provides a business and social network for its members.

Following the death of his parents, King Charles is currently the sole 'Grantor' and as monarch he has the ability to appoint others – most likely his Queen Consort and his son and heir, the Prince of Wales. When a Grantor dies or abdicates, the Royal Warrant becomes void but, according to the RWHA, 'the company or individual may continue to use the Royal Arms in connection with the business for up to two years, provided there is no significant change within the company concerned.' We can therefore expect to see products carrying the Royal Arms of Queen Elizabeth II until 2024, as well as those of the former Prince of Wales until the point in time when the insignia will either be updated with that of the new Grantor, or removed if the warrant is being discontinued. According to the RWHA, upon a change of sovereignty, the Royal Household will also conduct a review of all warrant grants.

Warrants are awarded to named company representatives, the 'Grantees'. Products or services need to be supplied for a minimum of five years out of the past seven, before companies can even start the detailed warrant application, a process which scrutinises

all aspects of the business, including its environmental and sustainability policy and action plan.

They are not granted for professional services such as banking, employment agencies or veterinary services, or to magazines, newspapers and similar publications. Other exclusions relate to goods or services provided to organisations such as Historic Royal Palaces, who manage premises such as the Tower of London and Hampton Court Palace, or the Royal Parks.

Applications filed by companies meeting the strict warrant criteria are submitted during May and June for detailed inspection by the Royal Household Warrants Committee, who after conducting all due diligence, make their recommendations to the Grantor. Between twenty and forty new warrants are awarded every year, replacing roughly the same number that are cancelled for reasons such as dwindling orders or company liquidation.

Successful applicants receive a formal letter from the Lord Chamberlain's office, followed by the warrant itself, an official document complete with embossed seals, which grants permission and responsibility for the display of the Royal Arms in connection with the Grantee's business.

Warrants are granted for a period of five years, meaning that resting on one's laurels in the glow of royal recognition is not an indefinite option. All transactions between Grantor and Grantee are conducted are on a commercial basis. Royal Warrants are not paid for by the Grantee and they receive no preferential treatment from the royal family. Indiscretion runs the risk of being stripped of their warrant. Memorably, the Royal Warrant for lingerie firm Rigby and Peller was withdrawn after one of the firm's directors referenced her appointments with members of the royal family in her published memoir. Warrants can also be cancelled at any time if he rules of use set out in great detail by the Lord Chamberlain, are not followed.

"You are informed on the extent to which the Royal Arms can be used in five different areas - your product or service, your stationery, marketing communications, company premises and your vehicles," explains Grantee Mark Platt, company director of Veritas Gifts, who offer a bespoke design service for luxury goods and accessories and who have been By Royal Appointment since 2011. "There are strict guidelines for usage, which are detailed in a document called the Lord Chamberlain's Handbook. Used on one ▶

Bags of Prestige

The handbags of longstanding Royal Warrant holder Launer were a staple and reassuringly familiar feature of the late Queen Elizabeth's working wardrobe. The company's worldwide recognition was given a further, unique boast when her handbag featured front and centre of the hilarious and endearing Paddington sketch introducing her Platinum Jubilee concert.

"A Royal Warrant is a sign of excellence, quality and patronage which Launer has enjoyed for more than fifty years," says Gerald Bodmer, company CEO. "It is highly treasured and was awarded in 1968 by Her Majesty The Queen, whom Launer had supplied with handbags and small leather goods since the early sixties. It's held in high esteem on an international scale and enabled Launer to achieve a high profile."

That the Queen treasured her Launer handbags was without question; one design from 1972 was photographed in its familiar position over her arm in the 1990s. The company's bags have also been favoured by other royal ladies, including the Princess of Wales and the Queen Consort, who carried a Launer leather clutch bag at her marriage to Prince Charles at Windsor Guildhall in 2005. The design of the couple's Welsh gold wedding rings was by another Royal Warrant holder, Wartski, who have held that honour from Charles since 1979.

of our gift boxes, for example, the Royal Arms has to be accompanied with the legend By Appointment to Her Majesty the Queen. Bespoke Manufacturer of Silver Gifts. Veritas Precious Metal Design Ltd Surrey on the prerequisite five lines, as specified to us."

"Essentially, the guidelines relate to privacy and discretion. For example, if you are at a trade show, you can't display a product which you have sold directly to a Grantor and advertise it as such. If we produced a product engraved with a royal cypher, we would not display it in a public environment. We also cannot display our Royal Warrant on the same plane as another logo."

Many companies have enjoyed Royal Warrants for decades, and some received their first centuries ago; Cadbury, for example, was awarded its first warrant in 1854 from Queen Victoria. Others, such as luxury gifting company Halcyon Days, have held Royal Warrants for all three Grantors at the same time.

For customers it highlights a good quality product and/or a trustworthy service, as reflected in the boost to sales it will invariably also deliver. For companies, the knowledge that their product or service is favoured by someone who has the entire national roll call of suppliers at their disposal, engenders a great sense of pride. It is, too, an extraordinary honour.

IMAGE CREDIT: SHUTTERSTOCK, LAUNER

"A Royal Warrant is a sign of excellence, quality and patronage which Launer has enjoyed for more than fifty years,"

From Henry II to Charles III

Royal Warrants evolved from the practice of awarding Royal Charters to guilds, the earliest remaining evidence dating to 1155 when the Weavers' Company received theirs to supply clothes and castle hangings to King Henry II. Over the next centuries the relationship between the Crown and individual tradesmen began to be recognised; 13th century records from 'The Great Wardrobe' detail transactions between the Royal Household and various craftsmen and traders, such as goldsmiths.

In the 15th century, royal tradespeople were recognised with a Royal Warrant of Appointment, one notable example being William Caxton, who became King's Printer to Edward IV in 1476. 16th century accounts detail the arrangements with one Thomas Hewytt to serve the court of Henry VIII with 'Swannes and Cranes' and 'all kinds of Wildfoule'. During his reign, it was the royal tradespeople who created the extravagant diplomatic meeting between himself and Francois I of France, known as the Field of the Cloth of Gold. Unsurprisingly, Oliver Cromwell abolished the system during the years of the Interregnum (1649-60), but King Charles II swiftly reinstated it after the restoration of the monarchy.

The Lord Chamberlain, as head of the Royal Household, would have appointed William Caxton, a responsibility that continued through to the 18th century - when Royal tradespeople first began to proudly display the Royal Arms on their premises - and which has remained to this day. After the ascension of Queen Victoria to the throne in 1837, almost 2,000 Royal Warrants were granted, including one to a Richard Twining, for supplying her tea. Twinings still proudly display two Royal Warrants today. During Victoria's reign, an association was formed to protect the rights of those who had been granted those warrants, an official step after years of informal, social gatherings of these tradespeople, to celebrate the queen's birthday.

By 1907, it became the Royal Warrant Holders Association, as it remains today. In 1990 the Queen Elizabeth Scholarship Trust (QEST) was established to mark the 150th anniversary of RWHA and the 90th birthday of Queen Elizabeth, the Queen Mother, to support the training and education of talented craftspeople and it has gone on to award over £5 million for that purpose. Since 1999 the organisation has also awarded the annual Plowden Medal to recognise significant contribution to the advancement of the conservation profession. •

THE OFFICIAL PORTRAIT MARKING
CHARLES' 60TH BIRTHDAY IN 2008.

A LIFE IN pictures

A COLLECTION OF SOME OF THE MOST
ICONIC AND MEANINGFUL IMAGES OF THE KING

WITH HIS DOTING GRANDPARENTS,
KING GEORGE VI AND QUEEN ELIZABETH.

PERFORMING A GUN DRILL
WITH SCHOOLMATES.

SEEN BETWEEN HIS GRANDMOTHER AND
MOTHER AS THE LATTER WAS CORONATED. ▶

KNEELING BEFORE HIS MOTHER AT HIS INVESTITURE CEREMONY TO OFFICIALLY BE CROWNED THE PRINCE OF WALES.

PARTICIPATING IN A TRADITIONAL HONGI IN NEW ZEALAND, 1983.

CHARLES MEETING WITH MOTHER TERESA IN KOLKATA, INDIA IN 1980.

WITH QUEEN ELIZABETH II AT HER DESK WHICH IS PILED WITH THE INFAMOUS DESPATCH BOXES IN 1969.

SAILING WITH FAMOUS BOAT DESIGNER, UFFA FOX, AT COWES IN 1976.

WINDSURFING IN MAJORCA, SPAIN WHILST ON HOLIDAY WITH HIS FAMILY IN 1989.

ENJOYING THE WATER IN 1978.

CHARLES CHATTING WITH WOUNDED MILITARY MAN, JOHN STRANGE, WHO WAS INJURED IN THE FALKLANDS WAR.

PROUD IN THE UNIFORM OF THE COLONEL-IN-CHIEF OF THE ROYAL REGIMENT OF WALES IN CARDIFF. CASTLE IN 1969.

CHARLES DRIVING A CHIEFTAIN TANK AT AN ARMY RANGE IN TIDWORTH IN 1985.▶

ON HIS WEDDING DAY TO DIANA IN 1981.

CROWDS GATHER IN THE MALL AHEAD OF THE WEDDING OF CHARLES AND DIANA.

ENJOYING SOME DOWNTIME WITH HIS SONS.

WITH HIS FAMILY ON HOLIDAY IN THE ISLES OF SCILLY.

TROOPING THE COLOUR WITH A BABY PRINCE WILLIAM IN 1984.

OFF TO ENJOY ONE OF HIS FAVOURITE PASTIMES, FISHING AT BALMORAL IN SCOTLAND.

FISHING IN LOCH MUICK, SCOTLAND WITH SON, PRINCE HARRY.

LIKE THE REST OF HIS FAMILY, CHARLES ALWAYS ADORED PLAYING POLO.

WITH PRINCES HARRY AND WILLIAM AT A POLO MATCH IN 1989.

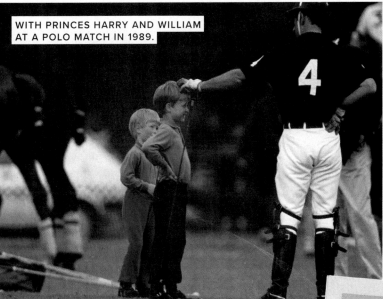

PICTURED AT A POLO MATCH.

KISSING THE HAND OF HIS MOTHER, THE QUEEN, AT THE CARTIER INTERNATIONAL POLO EVENT IN 1988. ▶

THE STATE OPENING OF PARLIAMENT, IN LONDON IN 1996.

ENJOYING THE THE BRAEMAR HIGHLAND GATHERING WITH HIS PARENTS AND SISTER IN 2017.

IN A CARRIAGE WITH HIS BELOVED GRANDMOTHER, THE QUEEN MOTHER.

WALKING BEHIND THE COFFIN OF HIS LATE FATHER, PRINCE PHILIP.

WITH HIS MOTHER, THE LATE QUEEN, TO MARK THE OFFICIAL PLANTING SEASON FOR THE QUEEN'S GREEN CANOPY IN 2021.

MARRYING A BEAMING CAMILLA AT ST GEORGE'S CHAPEL IN WINDSOR IN 2005.

AT THE PLATINUM JUBILEE PAGEANT ON THE BALCONY OF BUCKINGHAM PALACE.

THE LATE QUEEN'S COFFIN PROCESSION.

THE KING HOLDING A VIGIL BESIDE THE COFFIN OF HIS MOTHER.

HIS MAJESTY DELIVERING HIS FIRST CHRISTMAS BROADCAST AS KING.

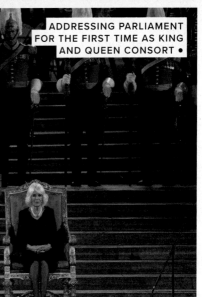

ADDRESSING PARLIAMENT FOR THE FIRST TIME AS KING AND QUEEN CONSORT ●

WORDS OF *wisdom*

WE CELEBRATE THE WIT AND THE WISDOM OF CHARLES WITH SOME OF HIS MOST IRREVERENT COMMENTS OF ALL TIME

"People seem to think they can all be pop stars, High Court judges, brilliant TV personalities or infinitely more competent heads of state without ever putting in the necessary work or having natural ability. This is the result of social utopianism which believes humanity can be genetically and socially engineered to contradict the lessons of history."

- A private memo written by Charles in March 2003.

"Something as curious as the Monarchy will not survive unless you take account of people's attitudes. The power always lies with the people. You cannot disregard their opinion and wishes if you want to rule them. It is they who have the final authority."

❝ What is wrong with everyone nowadays? Why do they all seem to think they are qualified to do things far beyond their technical capabilities? ❞

"Painting transports me into another dimension, which, quite literally, refreshes parts of the soul, which other activities cannot reach."

❝ Humility is to make a right estimate of one's self. It is no humility for a man to think less of himself than he ought, though it might rather puzzle him to do that. ❞

"There isn't really a set job or role. You have to some extent do what you feel is right. Doing nothing would be easy enough. The important thing is to serve this country and its people and the Commonwealth." ▶

"As human beings we suffer from an innate tendency to jump to conclusions; to judge people too quickly and to pronounce them failures or heroes without due consideration of the actual facts and ideals of the period."

IMAGE CREDIT: SHUTTERSTOCK

On family || At the centre of Charles' life is his family and he has spoken eloquently on the importance of those closest to him.

"As a father, I am proud that my sons have recognised this threat... (climate change) My elder son, William, launched the prestigious Earthshot Prize to incentivise change and help repair our planet over the next ten years...". He added: *"And my younger son, Harry, has highlighted the impact of climate change, especially in relation to Africa and committed his charity to being net zero."*

"If your children want to alter society, listen to their reasons and the idealism behind them. Don't crush them with some clever remark straight away."

Speaking about the attributes he hopes to pass on to his sons:

"Sensitivity to others, which by any definition is actually called good manners, which I think a lot of people have forgotten and also, on the whole, do unto others as you'd have them do unto you, which is not a bad way of trying to operate."

CO-PARENTING WITH DIANA:

" We discuss it, but that's a matter for us, isn't it? It's not a matter for other people to decide how our children should be educated or brought up, but you can bet your bottom dollar, they will all interfere and they will all say, 'It should have been done this way!' That's become a national pastime. "

"I miss my grandmother every day. I miss her vitality, her interest in the lives of others, her courage and determination, her perceptive wisdom, her calm in the face of all difficulties, her steadfast belief in the British people and, above all, her unstoppable sense of mischievous humor."

Watching his sons grow up: "As they get older, the more things perhaps they, being boys, can do with their father. That is obviously more and more enjoyable. But, I've always mucked around with them a great deal. When William was tiny, I used to muck around with him as much as I possibly could."

"Throughout her life, Her Majesty The Queen – my beloved Mother – was an inspiration and example to me and to all my family, and we owe her the most heartfelt debt any family can owe to their mother; for her love, affection, guidance, understanding and example."

ON HIS RELATIONSHIP WITH CAMILLA:
66 It's always marvellous to have somebody who, you know, you feel understands and wants to encourage. Although she certainly pokes fun if I get too serious about things. And all that helps. 99

Becoming a grandparent:
"Grandparenthood is a unique moment in anyone's life, as countless kind people have told me in recent months, so I am enormously proud and happy to be a grandfather for the first time and we are eagerly looking forward to seeing the baby in the near future."

On his wedding to Diana:
"Neither of us can get over the atmosphere... it made us both extraordinarily proud to be British."

"Relationships with fathers can be such complex ones... So often, I suppose, one must long to have got on better or to have been able to talk freely about the things that matter deeply but one was too inhibited to discuss." ►

"While the demand for organic food outstrips supply, we happen to know that 77 percent of consumers don't want genetically engineered crops grown in this country. Consumers can choose whether to buy organic produce. Genetically modified ingredients will deny us choice in the long run."

"I don't want to be confronted by my future grandchild asking, 'why didn't you do something?'"

"The simple fact is the world is not paying for the services the forest provide. Now, they are worth more dead than alive – for soya, for bean, for palm oil and for logging, feeding the demand from other countries. Speaking as someone from one of those countries, I think we need to be clear that the drivers of rainforest destruction do not originate in the rainforest nations, but in the more developed countries which, unwittingly or not, have caused climate change.

"This is precisely why I started my Rainforests Project, which has three main elements. Firstly, to determine how much funding the rainforest countries need to re-orientate their economies so that the trees are worth more alive than dead. Secondly, to show how this funding can be provided by the more developed world and, thirdly, to help identify ways in which the funding could be used in a durable and equitable way by the rainforest nations.

"There are moves afoot to develop markets that can provide incentives to reduce deforestation. But, this may take too long and we do not have the luxury of time."

"It is vitally important that we can continue to say, with absolute conviction, that organic farming delivers the highest quality, best-tasting food, produced without artificial chemicals or genetic modification, and with respect for animal welfare and the environment, while helping to maintain the landscape and rural communities."

"Forests are the world's air-conditioning system, the lungs of the planet, and we are on the verge of switching it off."

"We have spent the best part of the past century enthusiastically testing the world to utter destruction; not looking closely enough at the long-term impact our actions will have."

66 Fast food may appear to be cheap food and, in the literal sense it often is, but that is because huge social and environmental costs are being excluded from the calculations. 99

"If you think about the impact of climate change, it should be how a doctor would deal with the problem. A scientific hypothesis is tested to absolute destruction, but medicine can't wait. If a doctor sees a child with a fever, he cannot wait for endless tests. He has to act on what is there. The risk of delay is so enormous that we can't wait until we are absolutely sure the patient is dying." ▸

Being heir || Charles has often spoken on becoming heir to the throne and what that means to him.

"I think it's something that dawns on you with the most ghastly, inexorable sense. I didn't suddenly wake up in my pram one day and say 'Yippee, I —', you know. But I think it just dawns on you, you know, slowly, that people are interested in one, and slowly you get the idea that you have a certain duty and responsibility."

"I find myself born into this particular position. I'm determined to make the most of it. And to do whatever I can to help. And I hope I leave things behind a little bit better than I found them."

"I learned the way a monkey learns, by watching its parents."

Gardening || Charles' passion for nature and gardening is well known. He has spoken at length on his love of all things green fingered.

"I happily talk to the plants and the trees, and listen to them. I think it's absolutely crucial."

"Only the other day I was inquiring of an entire bed of old-fashioned roses, forced to listen to my ramblings on the meaning of the universe as I sat cross-legged in the lotus position in front of them." •

"We had a tiny bit at the back of the garden where we could grow a few vegetables and tomatoes. That experience is very valuable and I hope my grandchildren can have the same."